Puzzles, Parables, & Paradox

"From now on I will tell you of new things, of hidden things unknown to you."

Isaiah 48:6

Dr. Randall Feller

Understanding

PUZZLES

the Mysteries

PARABLES

of God's

& PARADOX

Kingdom

Cover Design by Blair Cruz

Puzzles, Parables, & Paradox by Randall D. Feller, Ph.D.

ISBN–13:979-8-9866261-1-6 (hardcover)
ISBN–13:979-8-9866261-0-9 (paperback)

Images from chapter 6 are from the Louvre, the British Museum, and the Metropolitan Museum of Art.

In honor of a life,
in memory of a special talent,
I dedicate this book to
Mildred E. Feller,
a gifted Bible storyteller
who made the Word of God
come alive in a young man's heart.

Acknowledgements

An undertaking like this book never happens in a vacuum. For every event in time there is always a context, a larger surrounding support system. As such, I would like to thank Linda Gray, my editor and proofreader, whose input, though sometimes challenging to hear, helped me to be better with my writing. I would also like to thank the administration of Oral Roberts University for allowing me a sabbatical to complete this work; the students in many of my classes over the years who have patiently listened as I shared the seed bed for much of this material; and the members of various connect groups at my local place of worship, Woodlake Church in Tulsa, Oklahoma, who have consistently encouraged me to place this information in writing. Additionally, I would like to thank my father, Robert E. Feller, whose many biblical discussions helped to shape my initial ideas for several chapters in this book.

Above all else I would like to thank my wife, who has listened to these ideas far more times that she would have preferred and yet who was still always supportive and encouraging. Without her love and constant companionship year after year, I would not be the man I am today, and I certainly would never have been able to complete this book.

To my children Laura & Joe Sauer and Nathan & Taylor Feller, I would like to say thank you for making me such a proud father. My fondest wish for you and your families is that you will fully embrace the information contained in this book and the lessons on growing as a mature Christian. May these mysteries shape your families' interactions with each other and may you be diligent to pass them on to your children.

And finally, for you, the reader: I am honored that you would take the time to read this material. May you find insight and wisdom to guide your progress in the Christian faith, may your understanding of the mysteries of the kingdom of God become a very strong part of your identity, and as such may you ever be faithful stewards of those mysteries.

Prologue

Hiding in Plain Sight

A good mystery hides strategic clues everywhere in plain sight.

I saw an interesting example of this when I was a growing up. A child was struggling to figure out a new puzzle he had been given. It was a rectangular wooden box with a secret. He watched with fascination as his father slid one panel after another until miraculously out rolled a shiny, bright marble. There was nothing particularly significant about the marble, but the suspense and excitement of discovering the secret of the Oriental puzzle box was captivating.

Wonder and awe turned to compelling curiosity. Through careful observation, the child noted that each wooden panel was stained a slightly different color, and each had decorative diagonal inlaid stripes that together formed a beautifully ornate piece of woodwork. Try as he may, the small rectangular work of art remained a mystery.

Curiosity gave way to stubborn determination. The key had to be the order in which the panels were moved, but there were so many. How did his father remember which to move next? After weeks of failed attempts, he had a moment of inspiration. Cautiously he moved the panel with a single diagonal stripe first. The panel with two diagonal stripes was second. With growing excitement, he moved each panel in order according to the number of inlaid decorative stripes. To his utter delight and amazement, the marble rolled out. He marveled at how simple the solution was and how obvious the clues had been. His joy at solving the puzzle was immense. To this day, it remains his favorite. Now when he looks at the puzzle, its solution is clear. But, when his friends pick it up, they are baffled. What is obvious to some remains a mystery to others. The key is knowing where to look.

Good mysteries hide strategic clues everywhere in plain sight.

So it is with the mysteries of God's kingdom. Here is a key question: if God wants all mankind to know him and his ways, why would he hide his wisdom in the form of a mystery? Why make his requests and demands seem so simple and straightforward to those of the Christian faith and yet appear to be unreasonable or even foolish to the rest of the world? Why speak through puzzles, parables, and paradox?

God is forever attempting to communicate with man. In doing so, he is as creative as he is determined. The same God who speaks through a still small voice thunders mightily from Mount Sinai. The same hand that gets a king's attention by writing on a wall silences a crowd by scribbling in the sand. The same voice that calls from a flaming bush quietly whispers its message of destiny through a soaking wet fleece. Whether it is through a valley of dry bones, a host of heavenly angels, a disturbing dream, or a stubborn donkey, God gets his message through. And in each instance God presents an unusual request, a puzzle of sorts, a mystery to be unraveled.

Through the still small voice, he commands Elijah to ask for food first from a raven and latter from the poorest woman in town. Through the thundering voice at Mount Sinai, he gives the commands and decrees that will guide the nation of Israel on a 40-year journey that should only take 11 days. The writing on the wall will condemn a pagan king for enjoying the spoils of war like any other conquering king would do. The scribbling in the sand will set a prostitute free who legally would have been executed. The flaming bush will demand that a single man—Moses—take on the most powerful nation on earth. The wet fleece will invite Gideon to fight a battle with only candles and pitchers. Each of these is a seemingly unreasonable request with what at first appears to be an impossible purpose. In the midst of these, God does not always expect understanding; he simply invites trust and obedience.

If God must choose whether to talk to you directly or to present you with a puzzle, which do think he is most likely to do? Which would you prefer? If he asked you to do something that seemed mysterious and puzzling, would you recognize his voice and respond?

What if he sent you on an earthly journey to find a city that did not exist on earth—as he did Abraham? What if he indicated that you would be the second highest ruler in the land and then sold you into slavery—like Joseph? Or how about giving you a dream that is vitally important and then making you forget it—as he did King Nebuchadnezzar? What about God's request for Hosea to marry a prostitute or his command to Isaiah to lie on his left side by the city gate for three months?

God is forever attempting to communicate with man. When it involves his commands and decrees, he is painfully direct. Do this, don't do that, live this way, avoid these things, and rejoice under these circumstances. The Bible is full of God's clear statements on how to live. Unfortunately, those clear statements are often in contradiction with our fallen human nature and what may at first glance seem right. And so it is not surprising that man invariably asks "why?" It is at this point that God's communication with mankind begins to appear fuzzy or cloudy, as if shrouded in secrecy. When we seek to understand his larger plan, he speaks of mysteries and hidden things. He purposely speaks through puzzles, parables, riddles, and paradox.

- Only occasionally does God speak directly of his plans: "When sharing his plan for Israel with Moses he spoke face to face, clearly and not in riddles" (Numbers 12:8).
- When revealing his plan for the nations to Daniel, he spoke frankly and then said, "Go your way because the words are closed up and sealed until the end" (Daniel 12:9).
- When proclaiming his plan for the Gentiles to Paul, he spoke directly and afterwards Paul states that "he heard inexpressible things, things that man is not permitted to tell" (2 Corinthians 12:2).

With the exception of these few examples, most of God's plans for man have been couched in mystery and intrigue. Although he has been direct and demanding in his commands and decrees, he seems to be elusive with his reasons and his overall plan. Even though the dos and don'ts of religion are clear and straightforward, his master design can seem elusive and unfathomable. And, amazingly, that is his intention.

Even so, to the person truly interested, his ways are not beyond knowing. In fact, he longs to teach us his ways (Isaiah 2:3), we are commanded to walk in all his ways (Deuteronomy 5:33), and he gets angry with people who have not known his ways (Hebrews 3:10). Although he often challenges us with the mysteries of life, of Godliness, and of his kingdom, he lovingly hides his answers everywhere in plain sight. His hope and desire is that we will be curious enough to find them. He pleads with us to go on a journey of discovery.

So listen carefully, think about these issues often, keep your eyes wide open, do not overlook the obvious, and try not to miss any of the clues that hide everywhere in plain sight. Whether you think about this at home in your easy chair, cuddled up by the fire, at work between projects, or in your car between destinations; consider this book a form of rough notes to the greatest mystery novel that the world has ever known.

Puzzles

God's Plan

"I speak to you in parables because to you it is given to know the mysteries of the kingdom of heaven, but not to them."

Matthew 13:11

1   Discovering God's Mysteries

Surreptitious Sleuth

Secrets, hidden treasures, the unknown, and mysteries have fascinated us since the beginning of time. They tantalize and tease. They bring out the sleuth in all of us. So much so that libraries, bookstores, and private collections around the globe are replete with suspense filled novels designed to capture the imagination and attention of their readers. From the most advanced literary critic to the young child just learning to read, without exception we all love a good mystery.

We involve ourselves in scavenger hunts, searches for lost treasure, childhood puzzles, mystery movies, escape rooms, and "who-done-its." We even devote entire weekends to mystery cruises. We are all—at one level or another—fascinated with the process of discovery. This is particularly true for young children. Sometimes as adults we become so bogged down in the affairs of everyday living that we lose sight of how fundamentally we are creatures driven by discovery. It is how we learn, how we grow, and how we become. So, in the middle of our busy lives, mysteries offer us a chance to set aside the mundane, to regain that spark of discovery, to become once again fascinated, to become like little children, and to revel in the search for the unknown or the unsolved.

Mysteries challenge the adept to solve their hidden secrets. Whether cuddling under a warm blanket next to a glowing fire on a cold winter's night or relaxing on a sandy beach, audiences the world over read with keen concentration, analyzing each new clue the author provides in the expectation that the mystery will be revealed, the clues will fall into place, and the solution will be made evident.

With this intense fascination for discovering the unknown, it is amazing that more people are not actively seeking to understand the greatest mystery the world has ever known. It is a mystery that—according to the Word of God—has been kept secret since the world began (Romans 16:25; 1 Corinthians 2:7). This mystery is interwoven throughout God's Holy Word, the Bible. In fact, its threads run though out all of time, human history, and the universe itself. There is nowhere in heaven or on earth that you cannot find bold clues to this amazing mystery. Like the stripes on the puzzle box, it hides everywhere in plain sight. So why do so many pass by the most amazing mystery novel ever written?

Sometimes answers are so close to us that we fail to see them. Have you ever tried to solve the mystery of where you last placed your glasses only to find after much searching that they were on top of your head, or even worse, the bridge of your nose? If you have ever had that experience, then you know what I am talking about.

Some of the greatest discoveries of science took years to accomplish because the answers were so obvious that everyone overlooked them. I remember sitting in an undergraduate biology class listening to a lecture on the history of modern medicine. The topic was germs. To people in our day and time, the idea of a "germ" is obvious. If disease is going to be passed on from one person to another, there must be some medium to transport the illness. This is a simple concept. But to the early 19th century mind, the outbreak and progression of disease was a mystery. They argued that nothing as farfetched as germs could exist and certainly nothing as simple as washing hands could solve the many problems associated with disease and sickness. The answer was too simple and too obvious. What made it even more difficult to believe for the 19th century mind was that the germs were "invisible." However, because mankind is "hard-wired" with an urgent need to know, to understand, and to solve puzzles and mysteries, it was not long before these radical ideas were tested and discovered to be true.

So it is with the things of God. Even though they are sometimes "invisible," the evidence and the answers are everywhere, and they are obvious. But often we overlook the obvious. We profess to be wise, but are we really? Do we see the many clues God gives us? Or are we so busy trying to find our own answers that we fail to notice his?

Why do so many miss it? Why does God hide his wisdom in the form of a mystery? Why go to such great lengths to keep things secret from the moment the world begins and then go even further to make them simple and obvious to us? Why hide things in plain sight? Why speak through puzzles, parables, and paradox?

Furthermore, if the mysteries of God's kingdom have been so well hidden for so long, how could a loving God ever hold us accountable for them? But he does hold us accountable. For his Word proclaims that all of creation points to the solution of this mystery. It states that "what may be known about God is plain to them because God has made it plain to them. For since the creation of the world, God's invisible qualities—his eternal power and divine nature—have been clearly seen, being understood from what has been made, so that men are without excuse" (Romans 1:19-20).

So what is it that we are supposed to clearly see? What are we accountable for? How do we live up to God's expectations? How do we understand the mysteries of God? How do we tap into the bold clues that are everywhere around us? How do we learn and grow from the process?

These questions tug on our hearts and minds. And make no mistake; our need to understand is strong. It is not an accident that we are a curious people. God purposely designed mankind with an intense fascination for solving mysteries. On more than one occasion Jesus gave thanks to his heavenly Father for hiding the things of God from the wise and learned and revealing them to little children (Matthew 11:25). He invites us to become like little children, to rediscover our sense of wonder and curiosity (Matthew 18:3). He invites us to go on a journey of discovery with him as our guide. He desperately wants us to search the secret things of God (Proverbs 2:4). He does this because he is the revealer of deep and hidden things (Daniel 2:47), and more than anything he longs for us to discover the mystery of his kingdom.

Mysteries pique our curiosity. They hook us and then reel us in. They offer us an opportunity to discover, and oh how we love that journey of discovery. It is built into humans by God to be curious about mysteries. They motivate us to explore and understand more of the world that we have been given dominion over. Mysteries are also invariably linked with fascination. Fascination occurs when our attention is captured by something. In the case of many mysteries, it is in watching the inevitable unfolding of events that help piece together the circumstances of the situation, the unknown factors, the principal players in the drama, the thrill of the chase, and the who-done-it resolution that all carry that fascination forward. Ultimately God wants us to be fascinated with the unknown, fascinated with the spiritual, and more than anything else fascinated with him.

People also love closure; they thoroughly enjoy resolution. As such, they expect the detective in a mystery to tie up the loose ends, they want the unknown to be clarified, and they hope that in the end justice will prevail. Because this is so, when all is said and done, the appeal of most mystery novels is that the reader is able to place trust in the author. He or she can feel confident that somewhere on or about the last page, the book is all going to make sense. The clues will fall into place. The mystery will be solved, and readers will have had a chance to figure it out ahead of time if they were really paying attention.

We trust the author of a cheap novel from an insignificant bookstore, but what about the Creator of the universe? In a world full of turmoil and so many unresolved issues, do we believe that God will give us closure and that justice will prevail? When confronted with God's mysteries, the meaning of life, his kingdom, or his ultimate plan for our lives, do we trust the author? We should! God says, "He will make known unto us the mystery of his will according to his good pleasure, which he purposed in Christ, to bring all things in heaven and earth together under one head, even Christ. In him we were also chosen, having been predestined according to the plan of him who works out everything in conformity with the purpose of his will" (Ephesians 1:9-11).

For readers who like to feel that they can trust the author to fit all the pieces of the puzzle into a brilliant solution, God assures us that (1) he has a plan, (2) he is working out every detail in heaven and on earth to conform to the purpose of that plan, and (3) although it has been kept a mystery, he has made it known unto us. God also promises that even though this mystery has been hidden from the ages and from generations, it is now being made manifest to his saints (Colossians 1:26). God himself has laid out a puzzle of sorts and asks us to approach this mystery with all the curiosity and sense of wonder that a little child has when exploring something for the first time.

Although in the natural there are many diverse kinds of puzzles and mysteries, over the years some of my favorites have been physical puzzles. By physical puzzles, I mean that there is just no way to solve them unless you start doing something physically with the puzzle. These puzzles that require physical manipulation come in many forms. Some you assemble, some you disassemble, some require navigation around hurdles or obstacles, and others require the fine motor skills of patience and balance. You can try all you want to logically go through the process of figuring the puzzle out. Even so, there is no substitute for jumping right in and actively manipulating the object itself. One puzzle in particular that I remember and enjoy is a box that can only be opened when two beads are lodged in their respective places on opposite ends of the puzzle's surface.

When attempting this puzzle most people start by tipping the surface to roll the first bead into place. However, when they tip the surface back to roll the second bead towards the other end of the channel, then the first bead is dislodged. Try as you might there seems to be no way to physically lodge one bead in place without dislodging the other. It appears at first as if it is impossible to get both beads at opposite ends of the puzzle at the same time. However, those who play around with the puzzle for any length of time finally end up spinning the puzzle, sometimes simply out of sheer frustration. When this happens, centrifugal force goes into action, and both beads then easily move out to opposite ends of the puzzle. Once you get actively and physically involved, you discover that the solution to the puzzle was much easier that you had imagined. Just like the Oriental puzzle box, once you know how to approach the problem, you will find the answer simple and obvious.

Again, we find that this is how it works as we approach God's mysteries. Jesus came to reveal the secret things of God that had been hidden since before the foundations of the world, He stated that, "I will open my mouth in parables, I will utter things hidden since the creation of the world (Matthew 13:34-35)". So through all four gospels (Matthew, Mark, Luke, and John) are recorded the many parables that Christ used to teach his disciples. Parables as taught by Jesus Christ were linguistic puzzles, metaphors for a more significant life lesson, and a revelation of some important concept that he wanted to reveal. On more than one occasion, the disciples asked why he spoke to them in parables. Jesus answered them saying, "I speak to you in parables because to you it is given to know the mysteries of the Kingdom of Heaven, but not to them" (Matthew 13:11), "so that hearing they will not hear and seeing they will not see" (Luke 8:10). Jesus was directly involved in the process of revealing the greatest of mysteries, but it was a stealthy and selective process designed to reveal the mysteries only to those who were really looking for them. But once you take action and you start looking, amazingly he makes the answers simple and obvious. Ultimately, he says to his disciples that unless you choose to get actively involved, you will never understand the parables or the mysteries. However, he was also telling them that if you will follow me and walk beside me, then I will be sure to help you comprehend the mysteries.

If we sincerely desire to understand, we need not fear that God's plan is beyond our comprehension because he has "given the full assurance of the understanding of the mystery of God" (Colossians 2:2). Not only can we understand this mystery, but also "through Christ we have become stewards of the mysteries of God" (1 Corinthians 4:1). "God wants to make plain to everyone the administration of his mystery, which for ages past was kept hidden in God, who created all things. His intent is that now, through the church, the manifold wisdom of God should be made known to the rulers and authorities in the heavenly realms, according to his eternal purpose that he accomplished in Christ Jesus our Lord" (Ephesians 3:9-11).

The Bible has one purpose: to reveal the mysteries of God's kingdom to man. He has gone out of his way by inspiring holy men from the past to place in writing the things he wanted to reveal. In fact, Timothy declares that "All Scripture is God-breathed" (2 Timothy 3:16). The creator of the universe intentionally took the time to intervene in the affairs of mankind to make the mysteries of his kingdom available to all. In doing so, God makes known his plans, his purpose, and the process by which he fulfills them in your life. And because this book is based on that revelation, you will see the same themes: his plan, his purpose, and his process.

So, what is this book all about? It is about a tremendously creative God disguising his plan for the ages in a mystery and then doing everything in his power to help you understand the mystery of his kingdom. It is about the God of clarity, speaking through puzzles, parables, and paradox. It's about an omnipotent God purposely hiding the secrets of the universe in plain sight. It is about a loving God going to incredible lengths to show you the obvious. It is about relationship, about trust, and about love. Most of all, it is about choice. It is about choosing to become actively involved and understand more of the mystery of his kingdom and what he wants for your life.

What does God want?

He wants you to see answers everywhere you look,
but only if you're looking.

He wants you to hear the clues and their meanings,
but only if you're listening.

He wants you to understand the mystery of his kingdom,
but only if you want to be part of the kingdom.

He wants to point you in the right direction,
but only if you choose to go on the journey with him.

"We speak of God's secret wisdom, a wisdom that has been hidden and that God destined for our glory before time began. None of the rulers of this age understood it, for if they had, they would not have crucified the Lord of Glory."

1 Corinthians 2:7

2   The Mystery Unfolds

The Game Is Afoot

In the beginning—GOD (Genesis 1:1). There is no mystery, no suspense, no subterfuge, and no intrigue. Neither are there any plots or counterplots, clues or foreshadowing, or hidden secrets. Only unity and harmony exist, for these are the essential characteristics of love; and love is alive in the form of an all-powerful, all-knowing God (1 John 4:8).

Then, ever so quietly at first—but with greater intensity as each new word is expressed—love speaks into the emptiness of space (Genesis 1:3)., and the heavens and the earth are formed (Psalm 33:6; John 1:3). Cherubim, seraphim, angels, archangels, morning stars, and all the bright hosts of heaven are created, each in their own due time (Ezekiel 10: 1; Isaiah 6:2). "For he spoke, and it was done; he commanded, and it stood fast" (Psalm 33:9). Time itself is brought into being.

The Earth's foundations are laid (Job 38:4). The morning stars sing together. The angels shout for joy (Job 38:7). Each of the constellations is brought forth in its season (Job 38:31). The heavens are filled with the music of life, and a majestic dance of harmony permeates all that is.

It is into this setting that God chooses to place his most perfect creation, and so a guardian cherub is formed. He is anointed and placed on earth in the Garden of Eden. He is the model of perfection, full of wisdom and perfect in beauty. Every precious stone adorns him (Ezekiel 28:12-13).

The music of the spheres is placed in him. As an angel of light, he shines brightly for all the host of heaven to see. He walks freely among the fiery stones and on the holy mount of God. He is Lucifer, and he is blameless in all his ways from the day he was created. (Ezekiel 28 14-15).

And this is where the intrigue begins. For Lucifer is blameless until the day wickedness is found in him. Because of his superior beauty, he becomes proud (Ezekiel 28:15-17). Because of his pride, he makes a choice to ascend to heaven. He attempts to raise his throne above the stars of God and to make himself like the Most High.

Even now, God could stop this sacrilege. He could take back the choice made by Lucifer, for he is the everlasting, omnipotent Jehovah. God does not have to let Lucifer travel down the path of evil. He has foreseen this event, and with nothing more than the voicing of a momentary thought, God could erase choice, pride, and sin. But choice is essential for the existence of love.

So God allows it. And Lucifer's path—the path of pride and self-promotion—becomes a significant element in the mystery of God's kingdom because his path makes that same choice possible for so many others. Even though it is not God's desire, it gives everyone who will follow the opportunity for choosing something or someone other than God. God allows it, already knowing how much it will hurt and what it will cost.

As a result, Lucifer, one of the morning stars, himself an angel of light, tries to ascend to heaven. He attempts to raise his throne above the other stars of God. His goal is to become like the Most High God (Isaiah 14: 13-14). But instead, he falls from heaven and is cast down to the earth (Isaiah 14: 12). He becomes angry; his wisdom and perfection are corrupted. Within him starts a fire that will eventually be all consuming and will leave him reduced to ashes in the sight of all who are watching (Ezekiel 28:17-18).

And only now is the stage set for the mystery to unfold. The essential elements have been conceived. All the forces of the drama are present—heaven and earth, good and evil, triumph and tragedy, hope and despair, as well as anger, hatred, and love. Most significantly, choice has been allowed to exist.

All of the characters who will act out this script are present as well—all save but one, man. So God says, "let us make man in our own image" (Genesis 1:26).

What happens next tears at the heart of Lucifer. It goes right to his core. In his innermost being, he screams out in agony as he hears God proclaim that man shall have dominion over everything on the earth—every seed-bearing plant, every animal, everything (Genesis 1:28).

The morning star who would have set himself above the other stars—this same guardian cherub who desired to rule the universe, this being perfected in beauty who declared that he would become as God—no longer has even one small planet to call his domain. Nothing is left but for him to become the prince of the rulers of the air (Ephesians 2:2). Caught somewhere between heaven and earth with no kingdom, no authority, and no hope, he is consumed by anger and revenge (Revelation 12:12).

And now the mystery begins in earnest. For God pulls together all these elements into a story that he conceived before time began. He places Adam in the same garden that he placed Lucifer (Genesis 2:8; 2:15). He also places the forbidden tree in the garden although he does not have to do this (Genesis 2:9). He could leave a perfect man untempted in a perfect garden, but God's goal is set on something far better than perfection. He sets his mark on the prize of love; it is his very nature.

So he gives man the same opportunity for choice that he gave to Lucifer even though he already knows how catastrophic this will be (Genesis 2:16). God has foreseen that Lucifer will use this as an occasion to gain back power and dominion. God already knows that man will make the wrong choice, so why would he allow such a thing?

God knows full well that Lucifer's choice—as well as man's—will shatter the harmony of the universe. Discord, strife, pain, violence, destruction, and evil will be the result, but God has a plan that is designed to redeem choice. His plan seems risky. It will be difficult and painful. It even involves his own death. Above all else, it requires absolute secrecy, for if Lucifer discovers the true nature of his plan before it is fulfilled, it will not work (1 Corinthians 2:8).

So imagine, if you will, God's dilemma. In order to redeem choice for himself, he has to keep his plans secret and not allow Lucifer to understand them. However, since the prize to be won is the redemption of human choice and love, it is essential that every man, woman, and child who desires to be part of his kingdom be able to understand his plan. How would God hide his plan in plain sight for all to see—all except Lucifer?

The answer comes back resoundingly as the mystery of God's kingdom. God will speak through puzzles, parables, and paradox. He will make known his plans in a way that Lucifer cannot understand. Lucifer's nature and desires are based on pride, power, mastery, rulership, and being like God. Therefore, God's plan will be based upon humility, servanthood, becoming lower than the angels, and taking the form of a man.

While Lucifer is busy searching for a king to conquer, a baby will lie gently in a manger (Luke 2:7). While the fallen star is striving to find and destroy the one who holds the universe together, a vulnerable little child will be held by a young Israelite girl named Mary (Matthew 2:16). At the same time, while the former angel of light is trying to convince the world that he knows more than God, a boy will stand in the temple confounding the priests (Luke 2:46-47). While the former guardian cherub is trying to tempt the Son of Man with wealth, power, and sustenance, the perfect Son of God will choose to forgo those things, live a simple life, and have no place to lay his head (Matthew 8:20). While the ruler of darkness prompts the crowds to try and force Jesus to become a king and overthrow Rome, a patient man will withdraw from the crowds to a solitary place and say, "it is not yet my time" (John 6:15). While the prince of the air is striving to be master of everything, the Messiah will take on the form of a servant (Philippians 2:6-7). While the evil one prompts even the High Priest to demand that Jesus clearly explain himself, the Holy one of Israel will speak in parables so that "while seeing they do not see and while hearing they do not hear" (Matthew 13:13). When the evil one who temporarily holds the keys to death, hell, and the grave tries to have the Son of God killed at all costs, a sinless man will willingly submit himself to the cross (John 10:17-18). While Satan rejoices in his apparent victory, the King of Kings will walk the halls of Hades, setting loose the captives and reclaiming the keys (Isaiah 61:1; Ephesian 4:8-9).

At every turn God will do what Lucifer does not expect. He will be the master of the paradox. To be strong, he will become weak. To be exalted, he will humble himself. To find joy, he will suffer persecution. He will give, in order that he might receive. He will take the form of a servant. so that he may one day be great. To be the great shepherd he will offer himself as a sacrificial lamb. To bring us healing he will be bruised and broken. As the author of life, he will be put to death. He will die to bring us eternal life, He will say to the young ruler, "if you want to be rich, sell everything you have." He will invite us to love our neighbors by being kind to strangers. He will ask us to love God by feeding the poor. He will say, "if you want to find your life, you will first have to lose it".

God will hide his plan in a mystery, a puzzle designed to be unsolvable by Satan. Satan's very nature keeps him from seeing the paradoxes, the kind of clues that God gives us. So God will flagrantly throw clues at us from a million directions hoping that we will stop long enough to notice. And in noticing, he hopes that we will understand his mystery and choose to love him.

"Now to him who is able to establish you by the gospel and the proclamation of Jesus Christ, according to the revelation of the mystery hidden for long ages past, but now revealed and made known through the prophetic writings by the command of the eternal God, so that all nations might believe and obey him."

Romans 16:25-26

3   **The Prophets Foretold**

So how will God choose to reveal his mystery to all those who are looking for it? How will God choose to share the intricate details of his master plan? Amazingly enough, the first thread in his tapestry will be his most bold; God will simply tell us outright. He will reveal every detail in a straightforward manner and yet do so in such a skillful way that it will still be kept as a secret from those not looking for the answers.

Have you ever been involved in piecing together a jigsaw puzzle? On holidays and family get-togethers, one of the things my family often does is puzzle building. Jigsaw puzzles are approached with a whole lot of fun and a little bit of competitiveness. With several doctors, educators, and a business office manager in the family, we have—as you might imagine—the whole process down to a science. Each doing his or her own part, we make quick work of the puzzle.

So what are the steps that assure us success when working with a jigsaw puzzle? I am sure you already know this process, but here is what we focus on: first turn all the pieces face up; next find the edge pieces to create the perimeter; and then, look for common colors, portions of an image, and also specific shapes. There are many clues to use in piecing together the puzzle.

With eagerness we each dive into our assigned tasks to quickly piece together the puzzle. Somehow, more often than not, I am assigned the midnight sky because my relatives know that I am good with spatial relationships. So while others have a range of clues for identifying the correct puzzle piece, I have to simply rely on shape. None the less, I enjoy the challenge. But whether one has many clues or just a few, what is the one thing above all others that helps with correctly completing the puzzle? It is the picture on the front of the box. When you know what the finished picture looks like, it makes a world of difference in your ability to piece together the puzzle.

So imagine for a moment, if you will, that someone would hide the cover of the box. What degree of difficulty has just been added to the puzzle's completion? On top of that, now randomly select pieces of the puzzle and divide them into 39 different piles. Some of the piles can be very large with many pieces. Others may have only one piece. Now in order to make this a real challenge, go to your local store and purchase 39 different jigsaw puzzles—all designed by the same puzzle master—and mix one of your 39 original piles of puzzle pieces in with each of the store-bought puzzles. Have we made it difficult enough yet to solve the original puzzle? Well, not quite. Finally, let us take several of the original puzzle pieces, find another puzzle piece that exactly matches it in shape from the store-bought puzzles, and print the image of the one puzzle's piece on the back side of the store-bought puzzle's piece so that the finished product will work equally well in both puzzles, depending on which side you are looking at.

Does all this sound excessive or too complicated? Would it surprise you to learn that it has already been done? God himself did just that in revealing his plan—the mystery of his kingdom—to mankind. The 39 puzzles are the 39 books of the Old Testament. The one special puzzle is the mystery of Godliness. And so, amazingly enough, the first thread in his tapestry is his boldest— God tells us outright. He reveals every detail of his plan in a straightforward manner but spread out through the 39 books of the Old Testament so that you can find it only if you are searching. Through the prophets, God reveals his plan of redemption. He tells us about the birth, life, death, and resurrection of the Messiah and what it means for all mankind. And so we will see that as God has stated in his Word:

- "Surely the Sovereign LORD does nothing without first revealing his plan to his servants the prophets" (Amos 3:7).
- "See, the former things have taken place, and new things I declare; before they spring into being I announce them to you" (Isaiah 42:9).
- "Declare what is to be, present it—let them take counsel together. Who foretold this long ago, who declared it from the distant past? Was it not I, the Lord?" (Isaiah 45:21).

- "I make known the end from the beginning, from ancient times, what is still to come. I say: My purpose will stand, and I will do all that I please" (Isaiah 46:10).

Subsequently, in the New Testament we see Jesus as well as the disciples reminding the followers of Jesus Christ that this process of redemption had already been foretold.

- "Jesus took the twelve aside and told them, 'We are going up to Jerusalem, and everything that is written by the prophets about the Son of Man will be fulfilled'" (Luke 18:31).
- "Indeed, all the prophets from Samuel on, as many as have spoken, have foretold these days" (Acts 3:24).
- "He has raised up a horn of salvation for us in the house of his servant David (as he said through his holy prophets of long ago)" (Luke 1:69).
- "Dear friends, this is now my second letter to you. I have written both of them as reminders to stimulate you to wholesome thinking. I want you to recall the words spoken in the past by the holy prophets" (2 Peter 3:1).
- "But in the days when the seventh angel is about to sound his trumpet, the mystery of God will be accomplished, just as he announced to his servants the prophets" (Revelation 10:7).

Revealing the Story of Redemption
The story of redemption was told in its entirety to those who were looking for it. How else could Simeon have stated at the dedication of the Baby Jesus, "Sovereign Lord, as you have promised, now dismiss your servant in peace. For my eyes have seen your salvation, which you have prepared in the sight of all people, a light for revelation to the Gentiles and for glory to your people Israel" (Luke 2:29-32).
So, if the story was hiding everywhere in plain sight and if it was prepared in the sight of all people, then why did only Anna and Simeon see it and recognize the baby Jesus on the day of his dedication? There were so many in the Jewish nation who had access to the many revelations of God and yet they were not actively looking to his revelations. Years before the prophet Jeremiah had

predicted that it would be so: "Hear this, you foolish and senseless people, who have eyes but do not see, who have ears but do not hear" (Jeremiah 5:21). In fact, Jesus directly told the Pharisees that were having trouble with his message that "If you believed Moses, you would believe me, for he wrote about me" (John 5:46). So, after his resurrection, when Christ was talking to the two men on the road to Emmaus, he said to them, "'How foolish you are, and how slow of heart to believe all that the prophets have spoken! Did not the Christ have to suffer these things and then enter his glory?' And beginning with Moses and all the prophets, he explained to them what was said in all the Scriptures concerning himself" (Luke 24:25-27). Jesus expounded what was said in all the Scriptures. So what Scriptures existed at that time? Only the Old Testament.

We also read that on many occasions when Paul preached to the Gentiles, the Bible states that "They arranged to meet Paul on a certain day and came in even larger numbers to the place where he was staying. From morning till evening he explained and declared to them the kingdom of God and tried to convince them about Jesus from the Law of Moses and from the Prophets" (Acts 28:23). Apollos also "vigorously refuted his Jewish opponents in public debate, proving from the Scriptures that Jesus was the Messiah" (Act 18:28).

The pieces of the puzzle had been there all along, but because they did not have the picture on the front of the box, it was hard to put the puzzle together. But we do have the picture. It is now clearly portrayed in the four gospels (Matthew, Mark, Luke, and John). As a result, we can—with confidence and clarity—put the puzzle together. And so we shall, beginning with Moses and the prophets.

The Promise of a Messiah

- *In God's first promise—speaking prophetically to Satan he declares,* "And I will put enmity between you and the woman, and between your offspring and hers; he will crush your head, and you will strike his heel" (Genesis 3:15).
- *To Abraham he states,* "I will bless those who bless you, and whoever curses you I will curse; and all peoples on earth will be blessed through you" (Genesis 12:3).

- *To the nation of Israel he decrees,* "Nevertheless, there will be no more gloom for those who were in distress. In the past he humbled the land of Zebulun and the land of Naphtali, but in the future he will honor Galilee of the Gentiles, by the way of the sea, along the Jordan. The people walking in darkness have seen a great light; on those living in the land of the shadow of death a light has dawned" (Isaiah 9:1-2).
- *He further declares,* "I see him, but not now; I behold him, but not near. A star will come out of Jacob; a scepter will rise out of Israel (Numbers 24:17).
- *Additionally he foretells,* "The scepter will not depart from Judah, nor the ruler's staff from between his feet, until he to whom it belongs shall come and the obedience of the nations shall be his (Genesis 49:10).
- *Through Daniel he prophesies,* "There before me was one like the son of man, coming with the clouds of heaven. He approached the Ancient of Days and was led into his presence. He was given authority, glory, and sovereign power; all nations and peoples of every language worshiped him. His dominion is an everlasting dominion that will not pass away, and his kingdom is one that will never be destroyed.

The Messiah's Birth
- *It will be a virgin birth.* "Therefore the Lord himself will give you a sign: The virgin will be with child and will give birth to a son and will call him Immanuel" (Isaiah 7:14).
- *The Messiah will be born a king.* "For to us a child is born, to us a son is given, and the government will be on his shoulders. And he will be called Wonderful Counselor, Mighty God, Everlasting Father, Prince of Peace. Of the increase of his government and peace there will be no end. He will reign on David's throne and over his kingdom, establishing and upholding it with justice and righteousness from that time on and forever" (Isaiah 9:6-7).
- *He will be born in Bethlehem.* "But you, Bethlehem Ephrathah, though you are small among the clans of Judah, out of you will come for me one who will be ruler over Israel, whose origins are from of old, from ancient times" (Micah 5:2).

- *There will be mourning after Herod tries to kill all the babies under two years old to get rid of the new king.* "This is what the LORD says: 'A voice is heard in Ramah, mourning and great weeping, Rachel weeping for her children and refusing to be comforted, because her children are no more'" (Jeremiah 31:15).
- *Being warned by the angel of God, Joseph will take Mary and the baby to Egypt to escape Herod.* "When Israel was a child, I loved him, and out of Egypt I called my son" (Hosea 11:1).

The Messiah's Life

- *He will grow in favor and stature.* "Who has believed our message and to whom has the arm of the LORD been revealed? He grew up before him like a tender shoot, and like a root out of dry ground. He had no beauty or majesty to attract us to him, nothing in his appearance that we should desire him" (Isaiah 53:1-2).
- *He will come with strength and humility.* "Here is my servant, whom I uphold, my chosen one in whom I delight; I will put my Spirit on him and he will bring justice to the nations. He will not shout or cry out, or raise his voice in the streets. A bruised reed he will not break, and a smoldering wick he will not snuff out. In faithfulness he will bring forth justice; he will not falter or be discouraged till he establishes justice on earth. In his law the islands will put their hope. This is what God the LORD says— he who created the heavens and stretched them out, who spread out the earth and all that comes out of it, who gives breath to its people, and life to those who walk on it: I, the LORD, have called you in righteousness; I will take hold of your hand. I will keep you and will make you to be a covenant for the people and a light for the Gentiles, to open eyes that are blind, to free captives from prison and to release from the dungeon those who sit in darkness" (Isaiah 42:1 -7).
- *He will come with good news.* "The Spirit of the Sovereign LORD is on me because the LORD has anointed me to preach good news to the poor. He has sent me to bind up the brokenhearted, to proclaim freedom for the captives and release from darkness for the prisoners" (Isaiah 61:1).

- *The Spirit of the Lord will descend on him.* "The Spirit of the Lord will rest on him—the Spirit of wisdom and of understanding, the Spirit of counsel and of might, the Spirit of knowledge and fear of the Lord. He will not judge by what he sees with his eyes, or decide by what he hears with his ears; but with righteousness he will judge the needy, with justice he will give decisions for the poor of the earth" (Isaiah 11:2-4).

- *He will speak in parables.* "O my people, hear my teaching; listen to the words of my mouth. I will open my mouth in parables, I will utter hidden things, things from of old" (Psalm 78:1-2).

- *He will see God's house as a house of prayer and not tolerate the money changers.* "...for zeal for your house consumes me" (Psalm 69:9).

- *He will heal the blind, the mute, the deaf, and the lame.* "Then the eyes of the blind will be opened and the ears of the deaf unstopped. Then will the lame leap like a deer and the mute tongue shout for joy" (Isaiah 35:5-6).

- *His triumphal entry into Jerusalem would be on the foal of a donkey.* "Rejoice greatly, O Daughter of Zion! Shout, Daughter of Jerusalem! See, your king comes to you, righteous and having salvation, gentle and riding on a donkey, on a colt, the foal of a donkey" (Zechariah 9:9).

- *The people will wave palm branches upon his entry to Jerusalem.* "Blessed is he who comes in the name of the Lord. From the house of the Lord we bless you. The Lord is God, and he has made his light shine upon us. With boughs in hand, join in the festival procession" (Psalm 118:26).

- *He will not be accepted as the Messiah even by his own brothers.* "I am a stranger to my brothers, an alien to my own mother's sons" (Psalm 69:8).

- *He will become a stumbling block for the nation of Israel.* "The LORD Almighty is the one you are to regard as holy, he is the one you are to fear, he is the one you are to dread, and he will be a sanctuary; but for both houses of Israel he will be a stone that causes men to stumble and a rock that makes them fall" (Isaiah 8:13-14).

- *Even though he will become the chief cornerstone, he will be rejected by his own people.* "The stone the builders rejected has become the capstone" (Psalm 118:22).
- *Even so he will become our strong foundation.* "So this is what the Sovereign LORD says: 'See, I lay a stone in Zion, a tested stone, a precious cornerstone for a sure foundation'" (Isaiah 28:16).
- *Because they cannot accept who he is, they will falsely accuse him.* "Let not those gloat over me who are my enemies without cause; let not those who hate me without reason maliciously wink the eye. They do not speak peaceably, but devise false accusations" (Psalm 35:19-20).
- *Without just cause, they will seek to have him crucified.* "Those who hate me without reason outnumber the hairs of my head; many are my enemies without cause, those who seek to destroy me" (Psalm 69:4).
- *The religious leaders will enlist Judas to betray him.* "Even my close friend, whom I trusted, he who shared my bread, has lifted up his heel against me" (Psalm 41:9).
- *He will be betrayed for 30 pieces of silver.* "And the Lord said to me, 'Throw it to the potter'—the handsome price at which they valued me! So I took the thirty pieces of silver and threw them to the potter at the house of the Lord" (Zachariah 11:12).

The Messiah's Death
- *He will die alongside two thieves.* "Therefore I will give him a portion among the great, and he will divide the spoils with the strong, because he poured out his life unto death, and was numbered with the transgressors. For he bore the sin of many, and made intercession for the transgressors" (Isaiah 53:12).
- *He will be beaten and mocked.* "I offered my back to those who beat me, my cheeks to those who pulled out my beard; I did not hide my face from mocking and spitting" (Isaiah 50:6).
- *They will hurl insults at him.* "But I am a worm and not a man, scorned by men and despised by the people. All who see me mock me; they hurl insults, shaking their heads: 'He trusts in the LORD; let the LORD rescue him. Let him deliver him, since he delights in him'" (Psalm 22:6-8).

- *The soldiers will cast lots for his clothing.* "They divide my garments among them and cast lots for my clothing" (Psalm 22:18).

- *They will pierce his hands and feet.* "Dogs have surrounded me; a band of evil men has encircled me, they have pierced my hands and my feet" (Psalm 22:16).

- *They will offer him gall and vinegar.* "They put gall in my food and gave me vinegar for my thirst" (Psalm 69:21).

- *He will suffer for our sins.* "But he was pierced for our transgressions, he was crushed for our iniquities; the punishment that brought us peace was upon him, and by his wounds we are healed" (Isaiah 53:5).

- *Even though the Romans usually broke the leg bones of those they crucified to hurry along the dying process, they would not need to do so for Christ Jesus.* "He protects all his bones, not one of them will be broken" (Psalm 34:20).

- *When they pierce his side, out would flow blood and water.* "I am poured out like water, and all my bones are out of joint. My heart has turned to wax; it has melted away within me. My strength is dried up like a potsherd, and my tongue sticks to the roof of my mouth; you lay me in the dust of death" (Psalm 22:14-15).

- *From the cross he will state,* "My God, my God, why have you forsaken me?" (Psalm 22:1).

- *He will also say,* "Into your hands I commit my spirit" (Psalm 31:5).

- *He will die for all of our transgressions.* "We all, like sheep, have gone astray, each of us has turned to his own way; and the LORD has laid on him the iniquity of us all. He was oppressed and afflicted, yet he did not open his mouth; he was led like a lamb to the slaughter, and as a sheep before her shearers is silent, so he did not open his mouth. By oppression and judgment he was taken away. And who can speak of his descendants? For he was cut off from the land of the living; for the transgression of my people he was stricken" (Isaiah 53:6-8).

- *His death would be gruesome.* "Just as there were many who were appalled at him—his appearance was so disfigured beyond that of any man and his form marred beyond human likeness" (Isaiah 52:14).

- *Even though he was to bring grace to the nation of Israel, they would end up crucifying Him and only later mourn for Him.* "And I will pour out on the house of David and the inhabitants of Jerusalem a spirit of grace and supplication. They will look on me, the one they have pierced, and they will mourn for him as one mourns for an only child" (Zechariah 12:10).

- *He will be stricken by God to carry our infirmities.* "He was despised and rejected by mankind, a man of suffering, and familiar with pain. Like one from whom people hide their faces he was despised, and we held him in low esteem. Surely he took up our infirmities and carried our sorrows, yet we considered him stricken by God, smitten by him, and afflicted" (Isaiah 53:3-4).

- *He would become our guilt offering.* "Yet it was the LORD's will to crush him and cause him to suffer, and though the LORD makes his life a guilt offering, he will see his offspring and prolong his days, and the will of the LORD will prosper in his hand" (Isaiah 53:10-12).

- *He will die like a common criminal between two thieves and be buried in a rich man's grave.* "He was assigned a grave with the wicked and with the rich in his death, though he had done no violence, nor was any deceit in his mouth" (Isaiah 53:9).

- *After his death, his disciples will scatter.* "'Awake, O sword, against my shepherd, against the man who is close to me!' declares the LORD Almighty. 'Strike the shepherd, and the sheep will be scattered'" (Zechariah 13:7).

The Messiah's Resurrection

- *Because of His sacrifice, he will be exalted.* "After the suffering of his soul, he will see the light of life and be satisfied; by his knowledge my righteous servant will justify many, and he will bear their iniquities. Therefore I will give him a portion among the great, and he will divide the spoils with the strong, because he poured out his life unto death, and was numbered with the transgressors. For he bore the sin of many, and made intercession for the transgressors" (Isaiah 53:11-12).

- *He will not be overcome by the grave.* "...because you will not abandon me to the grave, nor will you let your Holy One see decay" (Psalm 16:10).
- *Because he will live a sinless life, he will not remain in the grave.* "You, Lord, brought me up from the realm of the dead; you spared me from going down to the pit" (Psalm 30:3).
- *After his death, he will ascend to heaven.* "But God will redeem me from the realm of the dead; he will surely take me to himself" (Psalm 49:15).
- *In the process, he will set the captives free.* "When you ascended on high, you led captives in your train" (Psalm 68:18).
- *His sacrifice will tear down the veil between God and man and conquer death forever.* "On this mountain he will destroy the shroud that enfolds all peoples, the sheet that covers all nations; he will swallow up death forever" (Isaiah 25:8).
- *His submission and sacrifice will lead to being given all power, all authority, and an everlasting kingdom.* "In my vision at night I looked, and there before me was one like a son of man, coming with the clouds of heaven. He approached the Ancient of Days and was led into his presence. He was given authority, glory, and sovereign power; all nations and people of every language worshiped him. His dominion is an everlasting dominion that will not pass away and his kingdom is one that will never be destroyed" (Daniel 7:13-14).

What It Means for Us All

- *He would come to rescue us all.* "All kings will bow down to him and all nations will serve him. For he will deliver the needy who cry out, the afflicted who have no one to help. He will take pity on the weak and the needy and save the needy from death. He will rescue them from oppression and violence, for precious is their blood in his sight" (Psalm 72:11-14).
- *He would reveal himself to the Gentiles.* "I revealed myself to those who did not ask for me; I was found by those who did not seek me. To a nation that did not call on my name, I said, `Here am I, here am I'" (Isaiah 65:1).

- *He would come to bring salvation.* "And everyone who calls on the name of the LORD will be saved" (Joel 2:32).

- *He would sit at the right hand of the Father.* "The LORD says to my Lord, 'Sit at my right hand until I make your enemies a footstool for your feet'" (Psalm 110:1).

- *One day, before him every knee will bow.* "Declare what is to be, present it. Who foretold this long ago, who declared it from the distant past? Was it not I, the LORD? And there is no God apart from me, a righteous God and a Savior; there is none but me. Turn to me and be saved, all you ends of the earth; for I am God, and there is no other. . . . Before me every knee will bow; by me every tongue will swear" (Isaiah 45:21).

- *Through him all nations will be blessed.* "May his name endure forever; may it continue as long as the sun. All nations will be blessed through him, and they will call him blessed" (Psalm 72:17).

- *We will rejoice in his salvation.* "He will swallow up death forever. . . . In that day they will say, 'Surely this is our God; we trusted in him, and he saved us. This is the LORD, we trusted in him; let us rejoice and be glad in his salvation'" (Isaiah 25:8-9).

- *He will redeem us from death.* "I will ransom them from the power of the grave; I will redeem them from death. Where, O death, are your plagues? Where, O grave is your destruction?" (Hosea 13:14).

- *He will forever be our intercessor and high priest.* "The LORD has sworn and will not change his mind: 'You are a priest forever, in the order of Melchizedek'" (Psalm 110:4).

Although there are many other prophetic references in the Old Testament, these are a few that clearly demonstrate that God was declaring plainly for all to see his plan of redemption. He was spelling out in every minute detail the promise of the birth, life, death, and resurrection of the Messiah as well as what that means for each of us. Through the prophets, God magnificently details how the sacrificial lamb—who is Christ Jesus—would make provision for our redemption. Along with the books of Matthew, Mark, Luke, and John, you could call the Old Testament the fifth gospel. In reality, it was the first gospel. It was a preview of things to come that was prophetically written years before its occurrence. God's mystery is directly revealed to anyone who was willing to look.

The mystery of Godliness had been there all along as a fantastic puzzle, hiding in plain sight: "Whoever has ears to hear, let them hear" (Matthew 13:9; Mark 4:9). In fact, Peter made this statement regarding these prophecies: "We also have this prophetic message as something completely reliable, and you will do well to pay attention to it, as to a light shining in a dark place" (2 Peter 1:19). For though this is a mystery that has been hidden from the foundations of the world, it has been made obvious and available to all who are willing to search for God's wisdom.

"These are a shadow of the things that were to come; the reality however, is found in Christ."

Colossians 2:17

4   A Shadow of Things to Come

Epic Foreshadowing

We have seen how thoroughly God revealed his plan for mankind. Through his prophets, the Master Designer has intricately woven this bold prophetic thread of a majestic tapestry to graphically portray the story of redemption (the birth, life, death, and resurrection of Christ and what it means for all mankind).

If you or I were God, we would stop right there, sit back, take inventory of our handiwork, and with satisfaction declare this was all that was needed. But, as you recall, God's plan (his intent) is that men be without excuse, so that everywhere they look, they will see his nature, the story of redemption, and understand that he is working out everything in heaven and earth to conform to the purpose of his plan. And so, the Old Testament prophets' revelations are only one of many threads in the tapestry with many more yet to be revealed.

Libraries, bookstores, and private collections around the globe are replete with suspense-filled novels designed to capture the imagination and attention of their readers. From the most advanced literary critic to the young child just learning to read, without exception we all love a good mystery. Mysteries challenge the adept to solve their hidden secrets. Audiences the world over read mysteries with keen concentration, analyzing each new clue the author provides in the expectation that the mystery will be revealed, the clues will fall into place, and the solution will be made evident. In the majority of those mysteries foreshadowing is one of the primary tools that mystery writers skillfully use to move our thoughts forward and build hopeful expectation that we may yet solve the mystery.

Have you ever noticed how adept mystery writers are at using foreshadowing to give clues and insight into what is yet to happen in their stories? Creative authors have the ability to move our focus and attention forward to the coming events. Foreshadowing invites the reader to wonder what will happen next and keeps them reading to find out. By mastering the art of foreshadowing, a mystery author can create layers. They are able to skillfully tell a story to the readers in waves, eventually revealing to them the entirety of the solution to the mystery. It creates an engaging and interactive narrative that allows involvement and revelation while the story unfolds and then further clarification and assurance of all the answers to the clues upon completion. Foreshadowing can also add dramatic tension to a story by building anticipation about what might happen next. Authors use foreshadowing to create suspense or to convey information that helps readers understand the plot. Additionally, foreshadowing can make extraordinary—even fanciful—events seem more believable. If the text foreshadows something, the reader feels prepared for the events when they finally happen.

So it is with the mystery of Godliness. In a million different ways, God uses foreshadowing to tell the story of redemption, and his intent is to reveal the mystery to us. He will masterfully weave foreshadowing into every facet of the timeline so that no matter where you look in all of history, you will be directed back to his plan of redemption. His goal is to build hopeful expectation so that we too may become stewards of the mystery. So briefly, let us look beyond the obvious prophecies about redemption and focus on some of the more subtle foreshadowing that is part of God's mystery.

When we speak of mystery writers, we understand that the mysteries are crafted in the minds of authors and are written down on parchment. Blank pages come to life and begin to reveal the plot, counterplots, suspense, subterfuge, and intrigue. Through skillful writing, the authors use foreshadowing to reveal the clues or hidden secrets so that the story takes on life and vibrancy.

However, when we speak of God's mystery—although God has chosen in part to reveal his mystery in written form (the Bible)— more often than not, he writes his mystery on the parchment of people's lives. As the suspense and intrigue develop, he chooses to use lives to foreshadow events in the mystery of his kingdom. Through mankind's interaction with God and with each other, the Author reveals the clues and secrets that have been hidden since before the foundations of the world.

So, God uses people's lives as an archetype or foreshadowing of redemption. God chooses men and women who are willing to be obedient and then directs their lives in such a manner as to portray an archetype or foreshadowing of the birth, life, death, and resurrection of Christ and what that means for our lives. For example, let's compare the lives of Adam and Jesus Christ and look at how Adam foreshadows Christ.

- *They were both born without an earthly father.* (Adam was formed by the hand and breath of God; Jesus was formed in a virgin's womb by the overshadowing presence of the Holy Spirit.)
- *They were both given authority over everything.* (Adam was given authority over all of the rest of creation, and Jesus was given authority over everything for all of eternity once he humbled himself unto death for the sins of all mankind.)
- *They were both sinless.* (Adam was sinless in the Garden until he ate of the Tree of the Knowledge of Good and Evil; Jesus was sinless throughout his life and then died on a tree in the form of a cross.)
- *They were both naked and bore shame.* Adam was naked and ashamed in the garden after he sinned, and Jesus was naked and bore our shame on the cross.
- *They each made a significant choice in a garden.* Adam turned away from God in the Garden of Eden, and Jesus turned toward God in the Garden of Gethsemane. Both of their choices to turn in a garden had lasting repercussions for their descendants.
- *They each made a choice that affected mankind from then on.* Adam's choices and lived experience plunged all of his earthly descendants into sin and destruction while Jesus Christ's choices and lived experience lifted all of his spiritual descendants into righteousness and glory.
- Adam chose to substitute himself for God while Jesus chose to substitute God (himself) for us.
- Adam was the head of the old creation, and Jesus is the head of the new creation.
- Adam was created in the image of God, and Jesus is the exact image of God; In fact, he states that, "Anyone who has seen me has seen the Father" (John 14:9).
- Adam was put to sleep to produce Eve while Jesus Christ was put to death to produce the Church. In both cases their "bride" was to come at a significant cost.

As can be easily seen, the parallels are many and obvious. God was using the life of the first fallen man to foreshadow the life of the first perfect man. In fact, Paul states that Adam was a pattern of the one who was to come (Romans 5:14). However, God does not choose to do so with only one man. For example, let's compare the life of Isaac and Jesus Christ.

- *Their birth was pre-announced to their parents by an angel.* (Isaac was announced to Abraham; Jesus was announced to Mary.)
- *They were both a child of God's promise.* (Isaac was promised to Abraham; Jesus the Messiah was promised to the nation of Israel.)
- *They each were born through a supernatural birth.* (Isaac through a barren womb, and Jesus through the womb of a virgin.)
- *They both went up a mountain to be sacrificed.* (Isaac went up the mountain of the Lord in the region of Moriah; Jesus went up the mount of Golgotha.)
- *They both carried the wood they were to be sacrificed on.* (Isaac carried the pile of wood; Jesus carried the wooden cross.)
- *They both willingly climbed on the altar.* (Isaac to fulfil his father's sacrificial promise to God; Jesus as his Father's sacrifice for the propitiation of our sins.)
- *They each were miraculously delivered from death.* (God provided a ram to deliver Isaac; God provided the resurrection to deliver Jesus.)
- *Their fathers later sent for a bride.* (Abraham sent his servant to prepare Isaac's bride, Rebecca; God sent the Holy Spirit to prepare Jesus' bride the Church.)

Again the parallels are numerous and obvious. Because of Abraham's obedience, God was able to use both Abraham's life and the life of his son as a foreshadowing of the heavenly Father and his Son Jesus Christ. We can go on, and we will, so let's compare the lives of Joseph and Jesus Christ.

They were both highly favored and loved by their father. (Joseph was Jacob's favorite son; Jesus was God's only son.)

- *They each were despised and rejected by their brothers.* (Joseph's brothers were jealous of him and hated him; Jesus' brothers thought he was out of his mind.)

- *They were both sold for pieces of silver.* (Joseph's brothers sold him into slavery for pieces of silver; Judas betrayed Jesus for 30 pieces of silver.)

- *They were both tempted but refused to give in to temptation.* (Potiphar's wife tried to tempt Joseph; Satan tried to tempt Jesus.)

- *They were both unjustly accused and condemned.* (Joseph was unjustly accused by Potiphar's wife and put in prison; Jesus was unjustly accused by Pharisees and crucified.)

- *They each were patient in suffering.* (Joseph suffered in prison; Jesus suffered the crucifixion.)

- *Later they were promoted to the second highest ruler.* (Joseph at the right hand of Pharaoh; Jesus at the right hand of God.)

- *They each married a Gentile bride after being rejected by their brothers.* (Joseph married Egyptian women; Jesus married a predominately Gentile church.)

- *They both revealed themselves to their brothers the second time because they were not recognized or accepted by them the first time.* (Joseph accepted and forgave his brothers when they came back with their youngest brother; Jesus will accept and forgive the nation of Israel when they recognize him during the end times)

Yet again, the pattern for redemption is mapped out in the life of a young man who followed God's leading. As a result, we see once more the foreshadowing that points to Jesus Christ. God's intent is that wherever we look in history, we can find a foreshadowing of the sacrifice he would make through his only Son. So as another example, we can compare the life of Moses and Jesus Christ.

- *They both were hidden away in Egypt to save their lives.* (Moses was protected from Pharaoh; Jesus was protected from Herod.)

- *They both willingly left their home for the sake of their people.* (Moses left the grandeur of the palace of Pharaoh; Jesus left the splendor and glory of heaven.)
- *They both came out of the wilderness full of power.* (Moses after 40 years in the wilderness came with the staff and power of God; Jesus after 40 days in the wilderness came full of the Holy Spirit and the power of God.)
- *They both delivered their people from bondage and oppression.* (Moses redeemed the Israelites from their hard Egyptian taskmasters with the blood of the Passover lamb; Jesus redeemed both the Israelites and the Gentiles from Satan with his own blood.)
- *They both interceded for their people when God the Father's holy nature called for their destruction.* (Moses interceded for the Israelites when they corrupted themselves and worshiped a golden calf. Moses offered his own life on their behalf and because of his love for them was prepared to take their guilt upon himself and to die for them; Jesus interceded for the whole of humankind, took their guilt on himself, and actually laid down his life because of his love for them.)
- *They were both mediators between God and man.* (Moses was the mediator of the Old Covenant of Law; Jesus was the mediator of the New Covenant of Grace.)

In a significant piece of foreshadowing we can also compare the life of Melchizedek, the King of Salem, with the life of Jesus Christ. Melchizedek was a priest that Abraham honored and gave tithe to after he was able to defeat the four kings that had seized the goods of Sodom and Gomorrah and had kidnapped his nephew Lot. After his victory and the return of his nephew, Abraham was blessed by Melchizedek. In examining what is recorded about this priest we find many parallels with the priesthood of Jesus Christ.

- *They both were priests outside the Levitical Priesthood.* Melchizedek was from another kingdom called Salem and Jesus was from the eternal kingdom of heaven
- *They both were kings of righteousness.* King of righteousness is a literal translation of the name Melchizedek and Jesus became

the king of righteousness because he purchased righteousness for us on the cross.

- *They both were kings of peace.* Melchizedek was the king of Salem and Salem means peace. Jesus is the Prince of Peace, who one day will bring a kingdom of everlasting peace.
- *They both have neither a beginning nor ending recorded in scripture.* Melchizedek seemed to come out of nowhere and neither his parents, his beginning, nor his ending are recorded. Jesus is the eternal son of God, having neither beginning nor end, he is eternally one with the Father and with the Holy Spirit

In fact, speaking of the messiah David says in the Psalms, "The Lord has sworn and will not change his mind: You are a priest forever, in the order of Melchizedek" (Psalm 110:4).

We could spend much more time talking about Joshua, David, Elijah, Boaz, or Jonah and all the other Christ figures and how their lives paralleled that of the Messiah. Suffice it to say, God was actively involved in weaving another thread of the tapestry. He was foreshadowing the events of redemption so that no matter where we looked in the history of mankind, we would be pointed back to the birth, life, death, and resurrection of the Messiah and what it means for us all.

But how do we know that we are not just grasping at straws and that these parallels between men's lives and the life of Christ are not just mere coincidence? How do we know that this is intentional foreshadowing? I suppose the best way to know intent is to ask the author directly. God's Word itself declares that the Old Testament is a picture language that explains the events in the New Testament.

As a result, Jesus Christ was continually saying things like "as Moses lifted up the serpent in the wilderness, so must the Son of man be lifted up" (John 3:14) or "as Jonah was three days and three nights in the belly of a huge fish, so the Son of man will be three days and three nights in the heart of the earth" (Matthew 12:40).

We also can read that Paul states, "The law is only a shadow of the good things to come" (Hebrews 10:1), "These are a shadow of the things to come; the reality, however, is in Christ" (Colossians 2:17), and "They serve at a sanctuary that is a copy and a shadow of what is in heaven" (Hebrews 8:5).

A shadow is a fuzzy picture—you can sort of get the outline of the object, a rough idea of what it looks like but not the complete picture. So in as many lives as would be willing to follow his instructions, God was foreshadowing or creating a rough idea of what was to come through redemption. When the Holy Spirit moved on men of old to write the Holy Scriptures, it is very clear that both what happened and the reasons they were written down were for our benefit.

So Paul states the following:

Now these things occurred as examples to keep us from setting our hearts on evil things as they did. Do not be idolaters, as some of them were; as it is written, "The people sat down to eat and drink and got up to indulge in pagan revelry." We should not commit sexual immorality, as some of them did—and in one day twenty-three thousand of them died. We should not test Christ, as some of them did—and were killed by snakes. And do not grumble, as some of them did—and were killed by the destroying angel. These things happened to them as examples and were written down as warnings for us, on whom the fulfillment of the ages has come. (1 Corinthians 10:6-11)

Even though these things were written down for our benefit, if we do not read and know these Bible stories, then we fail to see the connections that are so important and so pervasive throughout the Bible.

In 1981, a game called Trivial Pursuit came out and quickly became all the rage. With information from categories like geography, entertainment, history, arts and literature, science and nature, and sports and leisure, there was a wealth of information in many different areas of life. However, to win the game, you had to know the trivia. You needed to be well versed in the facts or the stories across a wide variety of domains. And so it is also with God's mysteries. To fully understand the mystery of Godliness—just like the trivia puzzle—you will only see the connections between events and recognize the foreshadowing if you know all the details of the stories. If you really want to understand how effectively God uses foreshadowing to tell the story of redemption, then you must read a wide range of stories in the Bible. It is not enough to vaguely know about some of the Bible stories; you must be familiar with the details. I hesitate here to call this Bible trivia because the details are anything but trivial. In fact, they are significantly important for understanding the mysteries that we are to be stewards of.

So in wave upon wave through the details of many different lives, God was actively giving us previews, warnings, archetypes, and many examples of foreshadowing regarding things to come so that we could eagerly with a pure heart and with hopeful expectation approach the mysteries and what they would mean for us.

"In him we were also chosen, having been predestined according to the plan of him who works out everything in conformity with the purpose of his will."

Ephesians 1:11

5	**Produced and Directed by God**

Divine Drama

Over and over again in the Old Testament, we see human dramas, intricate portrayals of the events yet to come, portrayals of redemption, its impact on our earthly lives, and the resulting entrance into the kingdom of God. In fact, we could liken God's involvement in these human dramas to Hollywood productions.

Probably one of the most intricate and amazing pieces of the puzzle is a process of foreshadowing in which God uses the entire nation of Israel to tell us about redemption and the results that are supposed to follow. Consider the largest drama of them all, never exceeded in human attempts, not even by the acclaimed efforts of Hollywood movie producer Cecil B. DeMille: *The Exodus*. God's original production of the Exodus involves a cast of millions.

As we have seen, the Scriptures show that God was producing dramas with the lives of real people. When we think of Hollywood productions, human producers typecast actors to select those that are best at pretending to be someone they are not. God, however, does not like pretense. God, more than anyone else, is able to type cast perfectly because he knows the hearts of men. Therefore, exercising great patience, he would wait for the fullness of time when all the people he would need in his dramas existed at the same time.

Have you ever wondered why it took God 400 years to get around to rescuing the children of Israel from the land of Egypt? When Jacob was prophesying over his descendants and then again before Joseph was about to die, they both asked to be buried back in the Promised Land, and they reminded their relatives that God would provide deliverance from Egypt and lead them into the Promised Land as he had promised on oath to their fathers Abraham, Isaac, and Jacob. They were referring to a time in the past when in a deep sleep the Lord came to Abraham not only promising that his descendants would inhabit the land, but then the Lord said to him, "Know for certain that your descendants will be strangers in a country not their own, and they will be enslaved and mistreated four hundred years. But I will punish the nation they serve as slaves, and afterward they will come out with great possessions. You, however, will go to your fathers in peace and be buried at a good old age. In the fourth generation your descendants will come back here, for the sin of the Amorites has not yet reached its full measure" (Genesis 15:13-16).

This seems like a very strange reason to delay the deliverance of God's people. Since under the pharaoh's command, Joseph had been appointed as the second highest ruler in the land, why not just return to the Promised Land in a time while Joseph and his descendants were still in that pharaoh's good graces. Why wait 400 more years for a time when the new pharaoh would no longer remember how Joseph and his family had saved all of Egypt? Also why wait for the sin of another group of people (the Amorites) to become out of control. This is another one of the puzzles that reveal the mystery of God's kingdom.

If we can for a moment, let us use the metaphor of a Sudoku puzzle. In a Sudoku puzzle you complete a 9x9 grid with the objective of filling the grid such that each row, each column, and each 3x3 sub-grid (also called a block or region) have all the numbers one through nine in them. In a well-designed grid, the puzzle designer partially completes the grid so that the puzzle only has a single solution. Since you can only place a single number 1-9 once in each row, column, or sub-grid; the placement of each number affects the placement of all the other numbers. What we see in God's economy is that like the Sudoku puzzle; the placement of each event in history affects all the others. We also see that each of the characters in his drama must perfectly interact with all the other characters in order for God's dramas to reveal their intended messages.

So God patiently waited 400 years until he found a pharaoh whose heart would be hardened by miracles, he waited until he found a Moses who could remain meek even under the most trying circumstances, and he waited until the sin of the Amorites had reached its full measure. God was preparing to produce an incredible drama utilizing the entire nation of Israel. In preparation for doing so, he brings together all the characters in the script— never forcing his actors to pretend but patiently waiting until each of the characters' own behaviors and choices could be used to

portray the story he would produce. The exodus was a real-life drama of the life of a believer. It was a drama portraying that which would become possible because of redemption. From our spiritual birth to our final rest in heaven, the drama depicts a cleansing by blood (the Passover), forsaking the world (Egypt), a water baptism ("they were all baptized into Moses in the cloud and in the sea") and an infilling of the Holy Spirit (the water from the rock).

Paul explains this: "For I do not want you to be ignorant of the fact, brothers, that our forefathers were all under the cloud and that they all passed through the sea. They were all baptized into Moses in the cloud and in the sea. They all ate the same spiritual food and drank the same spiritual drink; for they drank from the spiritual rock that accompanied them, and that rock was Christ" (1 Corinthians 10:1-4).

The nation of Israel was miraculously saved from bondage and from death by the shedding of the blood of the Passover lamb, which served as an archetype of Jesus Christ's sacrifice for our sins. Then God fought their battles for them through many miracles, signs, and wonders as they fled from Egypt. This symbolizes the lifting of burdens and freedom that comes from a new life in Christ. When they passed through the Red Sea, it was a type of water baptism representing leaving the old life behind and entering a new destiny for their lives. Next, as they waited on God in the wilderness, he provided living water to sustain them and to empower them for their journey. This was the water that flowed out from the rock after Moses was instructed to strike it with his rod. This also is a type of the infilling of the Holy Spirit that is available to empower believers who wait upon the Lord.

Note that God fought all the battles miraculously for Moses and the Israelites prior to their drinking water from the rock in the wilderness. The children of Israel fought no battles on their own until after they had drunk of the water (Holy Spirit) from the spiritual rock (Christ). Again, this is a symbol or archetype of what is to transpire in the life of every believer. As we mature in Christ, we can be empowered by the Holy Spirit to take up our own cross and follow Christ. Then, as empowered disciples, we can be "soldiers of the cross," as the hymn lyrics declare. Notice that the children of Israel only began to fight spiritual battles in the drama after their endowment with this spiritual power. Their first encounter after that was with the Amalekites and Amorites, nations so evil that they were cast in the role of Satan in the drama. As soon as a believer is saved and baptized in the spirit, Satan will attack him or her to destroy their spiritual power with God.

It is interesting that many years later, God tried to explain to Saul why he should utterly destroy the Amalekites; he said that it was because Amalekites set up ambushes against the children of Israel (1 Samuel 15:2). Historians tell us that the Amalekites struck at the straggling, the weak, or anyone who strayed too far from the camp. This is an excellent picture of Satan. He attempts to ensnare, he attacks the weak and those who stray from the narrow path that God has laid out for them and is described as one who "prowls around like a roaring lion looking for someone to devour" (1 Peter 5:8). Since the Amalekites and Amorites fit that manifestation of Satan in their interactions with Israel and their sin had become so great, God gave them Satan's judgment (Exodus 17:16; Deuteronomy 25:17-19). God promised to fight against the Amalekites from generation to generation and to blot out the remembrance of Amalek from under heaven, just as God will fight against Satan from generation to generation and will finally cast him into outer darkness. The complete annihilation of the Amalekites— men, women, and children, together with all of their cattle—was an extremely harsh punishment that seems to be out of character for a patient and loving God. Even so, a longsuffering and holy God commanded this punishment because the Amorites and Amalekites, whose sin had reached its full measure, were so close to the image of Satan in their behavior that he could justly execute a sentence for the role they had played in the drama.

Another way we see that God was active in producing this drama is to examine his interactions with Moses, who—according to God—was the meekest man who ever lived (Numbers 12:3). Once the children of Israel had crossed the Red Sea and traveled into the wilderness, they became thirsty and started to complain. In response, Moses consulted with God. So the LORD answered Moses, "'Walk on ahead of the people. Take with you some of the elders of Israel and take in your hand the staff with which you struck the Nile and go. I will stand there before you by the rock at Horeb. Strike the rock, and water will come out of it for the people to drink.' So Moses did this in the sight of the elders of Israel" (Exodus

17:5-6). Since Paul tells us in the New Testament that the rock was a symbol for Christ and that the water was a symbol for the Spirit, we learn that Christ was to be struck once for the provision of his people.

Later in their journey through the wilderness, the people became thirsty again.

> Now there was no water for the community, and the people gathered in opposition to Moses and Aaron. They quarreled with Moses and said, "If only we had died when our brothers fell dead before the LORD! Why did you bring the LORD's community into this desert, that we and our livestock should die here? Why did you bring us up out of Egypt to this terrible place? It has no grain or figs, grapevines or pomegranates. And there is no water to drink!"
>
> Moses and Aaron went from the assembly to the entrance to the tent of meeting and fell facedown, and the glory of the LORD appeared to them. The LORD said to Moses, "Take the staff, and you and your brother Aaron gather the assembly together. Speak to that rock before their eyes and it will pour out its water. You will bring water out of the rock for the community so they and their livestock can drink."
>
> So Moses took the staff from the LORD's presence, just as he commanded him. He and Aaron gathered the assembly together in front of the rock and Moses said to them, "Listen, you rebels, must we bring you water out of this rock?" Then Moses raised his arm and struck the rock twice with his staff. Water gushed out, and the community and their livestock drank. Even though Moses had not followed God's instructions, for the sake of the people God still did the miraculous. This shows that although God sometimes goes ahead and blesses us for His namesake, He does not always approve of our behavior.
>
> But the LORD said to Moses and Aaron, "Because you did not trust in me enough to honor me as holy in the sight of the Israelites, you will not bring this community into the land I give them." (Numbers 20:2-12)

Moses was instructed to strike the rock the first time. Because the rock was an archetype of Christ, in the drama this represents the crucifixion of Christ and the outpouring of water represented the outpouring of the Spirit. On the second occasion when the Children of Israel grumbled and complained about the lack of water, Moses was told by God simply to speak to the rock. Instead, he became angry and struck the rock twice. This was a serious deviation from the Producer's script. God's drama was designed with the intent of revealing to us that the rock, which represents Christ Jesus, would be struck once for the sins of many and from then on we could freely ask anything in his name and it would be given to us. Unfortunately, in his frustration and anger with the people of Israel, Moses deviated from God's script.

If any man deserved to enter the Promised Land, surely it was Moses. After all, he was considered by God to be the meekest man who had ever lived. He was "more humble than anyone on the face of the earth" (Numbers 12:3). He was seen as someone who would not lose control even in the most trying of circumstances, and yet he did. However, because of his deviation from God's holy script, what Moses longed for most was withheld from him. He was able to bring the children of Israel to the Promised Land, but he was not allowed to go into it himself. This seemingly harsh punishment was given so that we would know that what Moses did was not God's intent.

Therefore, God's productions have been without equal. He wanted his audience (Spirit-led people) to clearly understand the important messages he was depicting on the canvas of real lives. We see in God's economy that like the Sudoku puzzle, the placement of each event in history affects all the others. Because he was a patient God, he would wait for many years for all of the pieces of his drama to fall into place. Once that time did finally arrive, he was therefore an exacting producer, with seemingly harsh punishments for those in the cast who did not perform according to his script. The result has been clearer insight into God's plans and purposes. God was portraying through the entire nation of Israel the process of redemption and what it would mean for all mankind. These events were produced and directed by God for our benefit, and as such he did not want us to get the incorrect message.

This is yet another thread in the tapestry, a scattering of clues, a foreshadowing of events to come, hiding everywhere in plain sight so that all who were looking might see. Whoever has eyes to see, let them see and "whoever has ears let them hear" Matthew 13:9). God was active in the life of a nation, painting a picture of redemption. Christ was to be struck once for the sins of many. From then on, we could freely ask anything in his name—another part of what redemption would provide as part of God's grand design.

"Daniel replied, "No wise man, enchanter, magician or diviner can explain to the king the mystery he has asked about, but there is a God in heaven who reveals mysteries. He has shown King Nebuchadnezzar what will happen in days to come."

Daniel 2:27-28

6	**The Kingdoms of This Earth**

International Intrigue

When we talk of earthly kingdoms, there is one that stands apart from all others in that it was the most powerful worldwide earthly kingdom ever to exist, and that God so uniquely interacted directly with its king. That kingdom was Babylon, and that king was Nebuchadnezzar.

We know from God's Word—the Holy Bible--and from many other historical accounts that King Nebuchadnezzar led the kingdom of Babylon to unique greatness. Not only did he conquer the known world in his day, but he is renowned for amassing great wealth, participating in great building programs, and commissioning great works of art. Perhaps he is most widely known for his creation of one of the seven wonders of the ancient world, the hanging gardens of Babylon.

King Nebuchadnezzar's Folly

Because of all of his accomplishments, King Nebuchadnezzar made the same costly mistake that Satan had made earlier, which led to his eventual downfall. He allowed his pride to override his reason, his behavior, and his service to God. It might seem strange to call a pagan king a servant of God. However, under the anointing of the Holy Spirit, Jeremiah had prophesied that—because of Israel's sin and continual turning away from God's precepts—God said, "I will summon all the peoples of the north and my servant Nebuchadnezzar, king of Babylon," declares the Lord, "and I will bring them against this land and its inhabitants . . . " (Jeremiah 25:9).

God himself had blessed Nebuchadnezzar for this purpose and had made him to be a great leader with many successes. Daniel, who was one of King Nebuchadnezzar's wise men and who also was his chief advisor, had warned the king that to not acknowledge God for his part in this would be catastrophic (Daniel 4:27). Even so, about one year after that warning, the king stood on his rooftop surveying his accomplishments and said the following:

Is not this the great Babylon I have built as the royal residence, by my mighty power and for the glory of my majesty? Even as the words were on his lips, a voice came from heaven, 'this is what is decreed for you, King Nebuchadnezzar: Your royal authority has been taken from you. You will be driven away from people and live with the wild animals; you will eat grass like the ox. Seven years will pass by for you until you acknowledge that the Most High is sovereign over all kingdoms on earth and gives them to anyone he wishes. (Daniel 4:29-32)

Not only had Daniel predicted this, but years earlier Isaiah had also prophesied that God would take this man who now ruled over the kingdoms of the Babylonians and the Assyrians and would punish the king "for the willful pride of his heart and the haughty look in his eyes. For he says, 'By the strength of my hand I have done this and by my wisdom, because I have understanding'" (Isaiah 10:12-14). Since God had blessed Nebuchadnezzar to use him for the purpose of punishing the nation of Israel, his indictment of King Nebuchadnezzar went as follows: "Does the ax raise itself above the person who swings it, or the saw boast against the one who uses it?" (Isaiah 10:15).

So for seven years, King Nebuchadnezzar wandered around like an animal, stark raving mad and completely incompetent to do any of the great things he had done before. Because of his pride, he was left completely incapacitated for any normal kind of life. Finally, at the end of the seven years, King Nebuchadnezzar's sanity was restored. Unlike Satan—whose anger continued to burn within him and ultimately led to his destruction, King Nebuchadnezzar finally acknowledged that God is sovereign, "that his dominion is eternal, and that his kingdom endures from generation to generation . . . that he does as he pleases with the powers of heaven and the peoples of the earth. No one can hold back his hand or say to him: 'What have you done?'" (Daniel 4:34-35).

What happens next is beyond belief, an amazing turn of events that has never happened before in the history of mankind and will never happen again. After seven years of insanity, dysfunction, wandering around like an animal, and eating grass, King Nebuchadnezzar's advisors and nobles sought him out and restored him to his throne (Daniel 4:36). It defies all human reason. No one elects a mentally insane man to an office of absolute authority over all aspects of their life. And yet that is what happened to King Nebuchadnezzar by the request of his subjects. In all of this, God's message was clear so that people may know "the decision is announced by messengers, the holy ones declares the verdict, so that the living may know that the Most High is sovereign over the kingdoms of men and gives them to anyone he wishes and sets over them even the lowliest of men" (Daniel 4:17). For anyone who might doubt that God has an active hand on the events of history, King Nebuchadnezzar settles the issue for all time. No one puts a man who has been completely insane in charge of everything. Only a sovereign God can or would even think to accomplish this.

King Nebuchadnezzar's Dream

All of this in and of itself would be amazing enough, but part of why God used his servant Nebuchadnezzar in this way was to reveal an even more amazing part of the mystery of his kingdom. So, God gives a dream to the most powerful earthly king the world has ever known. Then he promptly turns around and makes him forget the dream. This is another one of the many challenging puzzles that God presents to mankind.

In fact, the only remnant of the dream that King Nebuchadnezzar had was the urgent memory of having had an extremely important dream but not being able to remember what it was. Then because he is the most powerful earthly king there ever was, he immediately asked for the impossible. He demanded that his magicians, enchanters, and wise men both tell him what the dream was and interpret accurately what the dream means, all this under the penalty of death should they not be able to do so. In fact, his advisors said, "There is no one on earth who can do what the king asks! No king, however great and mighty, has ever asked such a thing of any magician or enchanter or astrologer. What the king asks is too difficult" (Daniel 2:10-11). Never before or since has an earthly king had that kind of unlimited—and seemingly unreasonable—power.

So when Daniel, one of the king's advisers, learns that soon they will all be put to death unless they come up with the answer, "Daniel returned to his house and explained the matter to his friends Hananiah, Mishael, and Azariah. He urged them to plead for mercy from the God of heaven concerning this mystery, so that he and his friends might not be executed with the rest of the wise men of Babylon. During the night the mystery was revealed to Daniel in a vision. Then Daniel praised the God of heaven and said, "Praise be to the name of God for ever and ever; wisdom and power are his. He changes times and seasons; he sets up kings and deposes them. He gives wisdom to the wise and knowledge to the discerning. He reveals deep and hidden things; he knows what lies in darkness, and light dwells with him. I thank and praise you, O God of my fathers. You have given me wisdom and power, you have made known to me what we asked of you, you have made known to us the dream of the king" (Daniel 2:17-23).

Daniel and his three friends were actively seeking understanding through God's wisdom, and God responded. God's Word states that you should "ask and it will be given to you; seek and you will find; knock and the door will be opened to you" (Matthew 7:7). Daniel, the king's advisor, had figured out that; God wants you to see answers everywhere you look, but only if you're looking. God wants you to hear the clues and their meanings, but only if you're listening. But once you do look or you dare to ask, God responds.

So then Daniel began to share the revelation from God with King Nebuchadnezzar:

> You looked, O King, and there before you stood a large statue—an enormous, dazzling statue, awesome in appearance. The head of the statue was made of pure gold, its chest and arms of silver, its belly and thighs of bronze, its legs of iron, its feet partly of iron and partly of baked clay. While you were watching, a rock was cut out, but not by human hands. It struck the statue on its feet of iron and clay and smashed them. Then the iron, the clay, the bronze, the silver and the gold were broken to pieces at the same time and became like chaff on a threshing floor in the summer. The wind swept them away without leaving a trace. But the rock that struck the statue became a huge mountain and filled the whole earth.
>
> This was the dream, and now we will interpret it to the king. You, O king, are the king of kings. The God of heaven has given you dominion and power and might and glory; in your hands he has placed mankind and the beasts of the field and the birds of the air. Wherever they live, he has made you ruler over them all. You are that head of gold.

After you, another kingdom will rise, inferior to yours. Next, a third kingdom, one of bronze, will rule over the whole earth. Finally, there will be a fourth kingdom, strong as iron--for iron breaks and smashes everything—and as iron breaks things to pieces, so it will crush and break all the others. Just as you saw that the feet and toes were partly of baked clay and partly of iron, so this will be a divided kingdom; yet it will have some of the strength of iron in it, even as you saw iron mixed with clay. As the toes were partly iron and partly clay, so this kingdom will be partly strong and partly brittle. And just as you saw the iron mixed with baked clay, so the people will be a mixture and will not remain united, any more than iron mixes with clay.

In the time of those kings, the God of heaven will set up a kingdom that will never be destroyed, nor will it be left to another people. It will crush all those kingdoms and bring them to an end, but it will itself endure forever. This is the meaning of the vision of the rock cut out of a mountain, but not by human hands—a rock that broke the iron, the bronze, the clay, the silver and the gold to pieces. The great God has shown the king what will take place in the future. The dream is true, and the interpretation is trustworthy. (Daniel 2:31-45)

As a result of this revelation, we see that God was prophetically revealing a succession of kingdoms and what was yet to come in this world—if you will, an international intrigue of worldwide kingdoms that would ultimately lead to one final kingdom that would never end. So King Nebuchadnezzar was satisfied with the telling of the dream and its interpretation and, as a result, elevated Daniel in his kingdom.

Daniel, however, being a very learned and wise man, considered these prophetic kingdoms with great curiosity. As such, he continued to ask God more and more about what this all meant. Why had the succession of kingdoms been revealed to the king? What was the purpose and meaning of the final eternal kingdom? As has been stated before, we are hard wired with curiosity and a fascination with puzzles and mysteries. To completely understand the book of Daniel in the Bible, you must recognize that it is a recounting of Daniel's journey of discovery in seeking the answers to those questions.

Daniel's Quest

The Bible says, "If any of you lacks wisdom, you should ask God, who gives generously to all without finding fault, and it will be given you" (James 1:5). Daniel had discovered this to be true in his own personal devotional times. He had also read in Jeremiah that God had said, "Call to me, and I will answer you and will tell you great and hidden things that you have not known" (Jeremiah 33:3). So through prayer and fasting, he started to pursue the mystery of this succession of kingdoms that had been revealed by God. Daniel, like King Nebuchadnezzar, now knew that there would be four worldwide kingdoms, each represented by a different type of metal and each with less authority and power than the previous kingdom. Then finally there would be a kingdom that comes from heaven and wipes out all the others. This final kingdom would start out small but then grow to fill the whole earth. While king Nebuchadnezzar would be satisfied that God had called the kingdom of Babylon the head of gold and the strongest kingdom, Daniel wanted to know more about the kingdoms to come.

We read in chapter seven of Daniel that in response to his searching and his prayers, Daniel was given a vision where he saw four beasts: (1) a winged lion that stood up on two feet and was given the mind of a man, (2) a bear raised up on one side with three ribs in its mouth, (3) a leopard with four wings on its back and four heads, and (4) a terrifying beast with iron teeth and with ten horns on its head. Finally, in his vision, Daniel saw one "like a Son of Man coming with the clouds of heaven," who was given authority, glory, and sovereign power, and all nations and people of every language worshiped him.

Because of the strangeness of the dream, Daniel asked for the meaning of all this. In response, he was told that the four beasts were the same four kingdoms that had been represented by different metals in King Nebuchadnezzar's dream but that the holy people of the Most High will receive the final kingdom and will possess it forever.

In his quest to understand more, Daniel continued to pray and had yet another vision, which was recorded in chapter eight. In this vision, Daniel saw a ram with two horns, one that was longer than the other that charged in all directions, and no one could stand before it. Then he saw a goat with one prominent horn that furiously attacked the ram, shattering its two horns. The ram became very great, but at the height of its power, the horn was broken off, and in its place four prominent horns grew.

Again, because the vision was so strange, a voice called for the angel Gabriel to explain the meaning to Daniel. So he revealed to Daniel that the two-horned ram was the same as the shoulders of silver in Nebuchadnezzar's dream as well as the bear risen up on one side in Daniel's previous vision and that this was going to be the kingdom of the Medes and the Persians. He also revealed that the goat with one prominent horn represented the same thing as the belly and thighs of bronze in King Nebuchadnezzar's dream—likewise the leopard with four wings and four heads in Daniel's previous vision. Gabriel also revealed that the one prominent horn would be the first king of that kingdom and that when it was broken off would be replaced by four other kings, who each were not as strong as the original king.

So we see in these three visions or dreams that God was communicating his plan for the succession of kingdoms through four major kingdoms and then finally a fifth and final kingdom that would come down out of heaven. Each vision gave increasing detail to enhance Daniel's understanding. God was revealing from his vantage point how he saw the authority given to each of the kingdoms. By using the symbols of gold, silver, bronze, and iron and finally the "rock not hewn by human hands," God was explaining the type of rule and authority each kingdom would have. As we progress down the statue's body through the different elements, we start with the most precious and move to the least precious of the elements.

So, in Babylon (represented by gold) the king had absolute authority. Only exactly what King Nebuchadnezzar said from moment to moment was followed, which is why one moment he could say, "throw the three Hebrew children in the fiery furnace," and the next moment he could countermand his own directive and say, "take them back out" (Daniel 3:20-26).

In the Medo-Persian Empire (represented by silver) once a command was set in law, it could not be changed, which was why King Darius was greatly grieved when his friend Daniel had to be thrown into the lion's den based on a law Darius had just enacted. As a result, even though he was the king, he had to wait until morning to see if his friend Daniel had survived (Daniel 6:14-20).

In the Greek Empire (represented by bronze) the only authority was by military might, but that authority never made it past military authority into political rule or public law.

Then the Roman Empire (represented by iron) was ruled by the caesars and the senate. Under the caesars, Roman government was more of a very rough or early form of a republic where different classes of citizens had varying degrees of impact on the voting for representatives. As a result, the authority was much more diffuse than—and, therefore, not as strong as—any of the previous empires. This remained true even through its tumultuous transition from an early republic to a Roman Empire.

Finally in the kingdom of heaven (represented by a rock not hewn by human hands) we see a kingdom whose authority is absolute and everlasting. Even though a rock is the least precious of all the elements, we read over and over in God's Word that the last shall be first and the least shall be the greatest. If you recall from earlier in this book, we recognize that the "rock" was Christ Jesus. Jesus had come in humility, as a servant of all, even sacrificing his life for others. As a result, he later was elevated by his heavenly Father. So once again, we are brought back to the central focus of God's plan, which was redemption though Jesus Christ and his resulting kingdom that would grow to fill the whole earth.

When most people approach the book of Daniel, similarly to the book of Revelation, all the images and visions seem too abstract or symbolic to fully understand. As a result, far too often readers skip over these books in the Bible, assuming that they are too difficult to comprehend. However, it has been my experience that with just a little effort, they are far more direct and understandable that at first thought. So how do we actually know that God is speaking in these visions of the kingdoms of Babylon, the Medo-Persians, the Greeks, and the Romans? Imagine my surprise when I was in college taking an art history course and found that the seemingly abstract symbols recorded in the book of Daniel were, in fact, fairly literal examples of the art and culture of each of the kingdoms. Therefore, just for a while, let us examine these three revelations to see what is being communicated and how it is revealed.

First, King Nebuchadnezzar's kingdom, the kingdom of Babylon, was represented by a head of gold and by a winged lion that stands on two feet and has the mind of a man. When you look at the art history of the Babylonian Empire, you see that their coinage and currency was actually gold. On their coins, one side was embossed with the image of Nebuchadnezzar and the other side with a picture of a lion. When you look at the columns and palisades of the architecture in Babylon, you see majestic lions with large sweeping wings and the head of a man in the image of King Nebuchadnezzar. In fact, in several carved reliefs, you also see a lion standing on its hind feet opposite a standing man who is also carved in the image of King Nebuchadnezzar. Finally, not only does all the art and culture of Babylon directly represent the images in the vision, but God's interpretation of the dream directly states that this represents Nebuchadnezzar's kingdom (Daniel 2:37).

Figure 1: Art, statuary, and gold coins of Babylon

Second, the kingdom of the Medes and the Persians was represented by the statue's chest and arms of silver, by a bear on its side with ribs in its teeth, and by a two-horned ram where one horn was much more prominent that the other. Just as with the first kingdom, the coinage matched the metal described in the vision. The principal coins of their empire were silver. Some of their coins literally have the face of a bear opposite the face of a ram. Additionally the bear and the ram images are painted on their pottery, sculpted on their knife and sword hilts, and carved into their chalices (drinking vessels), furniture, and ornate decorative pieces. The bear lifted up on one side. and the two horns of the ram—with one more prominent than the other—also show the nature of the Medo-Persian Empire. The empire was a coalition of two kingdoms; the Medes were known for their intelligence and strategy, and the Persians were known for their military might. Together they were able to overcome the Babylonian Empire and take over the territories of the known world. So the bear lifted up on one side and the two horns, one larger than the other, show this lopsided alliance. Finally, the angel Gabriel directly told Daniel that the two horns of the ram represent the kings of Media and Persia (Daniel 8:20).

Figure 2: Art, statuary, and silver coins of Medo-Persia

Next the kingdom of Greece was represented by the statue's belly and thighs of bronze, by a leopard with four wings and four heads, and by a goat with one prominent horn that is cut off with four horns growing in its place. Once again, the coinage of the kingdom of Greece is made of the bronze metal seen in Nebuchadnezzar's dream. Carved in these coins is a side view of Alexander the Great, who is always shown with one prominent goat's horn coming out of his head. Additionally during his conquests, he likened himself to a leopard, strong and swift. This was so much a part of the national identity that we see the leopard repeatedly featured in the artwork of their bronze platters, the carvings in their pottery, and the sculpting of their statuary. The one prominent horn cut off and replaced with four weaker horns becomes self-evident when you read how when Alexander the Great reached the pinnacle of his military conquests, his four generals killed him and divided his kingdom among them. As a result, the four wings and four heads of the leopard as well as the four horns of the goat are representative of the four final leaders of this third kingdom of Greece.

Figure 3: Art, statuary, and bronze coins of Greece

The last of the four earthly kingdoms is represented by the statue's legs of iron, feet of mixed iron and clay, and a terrifying beast that trampled everything underfoot. Looking at the coinage of the Roman Empire, we see a mixture of different types of metal. While they did use the coins of all the prior empires, the silver and bronze in particular were fairly soft metals. As a result, the Romans would use their strong iron to make "dies" with which they could easily stamp the image of Caesar into the soft, precious metals, thereby repurposing the previous kingdom's coinage. Most significantly their weapons and tools were made of iron. Although they were not as valuable as the gold, silver, and bronze, they were much stronger and helped the armies of Rome trample all the other nations underfoot. In addition, a big part of their statuary and carvings were focused on the legendary story of Romulus and Remus, who were raised by a she-wolf that was described as a terrible beast. According to the legend, they decided to build a city where the beast had found them. As the brothers quarreled over where that site would be, Romulus ended up killing his brother Remus, which left him the sole founder of the new city of Rome. So even though it was just a legend, Romans taught their children that the city of Rome—and thus the Roman Empire—was birthed quickly out of betrayal and violence and became an empire that devoured its victims and trampled underfoot whatever was left. This history of violence, betrayal, and trampling underfoot also gets played out in the succession of caesars and their senates.

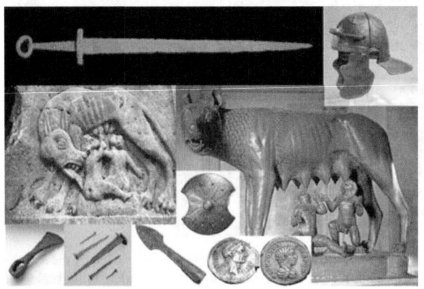

Figure 4: Art, iron works, and iron-pressed coins of Rome

The timing and nature of these four kingdoms had been revealed to Daniel by God because of his earnest desire to know and his willingness to ask God directly. With his passion for understanding God's wisdom and with each new subsequent revelation, he had also acquired an unprecedented insight into many things yet to come. Even so, he still struggled to understand more.

Have you ever tried to solve a Rubik's Cube? It is a classic permutation puzzle whose object is to rearrange the pieces into a target configuration where the sections on the face of each side are all one color. At first glance the cube is deceptively simple. The true challenge of solving a Rubik's Cube is that there are more than 43 quintillion potential variations. To master the cube, you must learn a sequence of movements that can be performed in successive order. The sequence of moves is critical to solving the cube. All moves must fall in the proper order for a particular section to arrive on a face of the cube as desired. Repeatedly this must be done throughout the process of solving the cube without undoing all the previous sections. Would it surprise you to learn that God has done just that with all the kingdoms of this earth, moving each to its proper place and time in order to accomplish his desire? God was purposely revealing through the story of king Nebuchadnezzar how he places in power those whom he wills in order so that they fall in proper sequence and his plans will be fulfilled.

Understanding the Final Worldwide Kingdom

Daniel was being given insight into how God was actively involved in this succession of kingdoms to bring about his designs on history. Because of his avid study of God's Word, he understood that "according to the Word of the Lord given to Jeremiah the prophet, that the desolation of Jerusalem would last seventy years" (Daniel 9:2). Jeremiah had prophesied that the "country would become a desolate waste land, and these nations would serve the king of Babylon seventy years" (Jeremiah 25:11). Since Daniel had already been in captivity that long, he pleaded with the Lord and petitioned him for understanding "in fasting, and in sackcloth and ashes" (Daniel 9:3). While he was still praying, the angel Gabriel came to him in answer to his prayer:

Seventy "sevens" are decreed for your people and your holy city to finish transgression, to put an end to sin, to atone for wickedness, and to bring everlasting righteousness, to seal up vision and prophesy and to anoint the Most Holy Place. Know and understand this: From the issuing of the decree to restore and rebuild Jerusalem until the Anointed One, the ruler, comes, there will be seven "sevens," and 62 "sevens," It will be rebuilt with streets and a trench, but in times of trouble. After the 62 "sevens," the Anointed One will be cut off and will have nothing." (Daniel 9:24-26)

All of this brings us to the final kingdom in King Nebuchadnezzar's dream, which would be an everlasting kingdom. The rock not hewn by human hands that would come down out of heaven, this same rock that would break up all the other kingdoms, this holy rock that would grow to become a kingdom that would fill the whole earth, this "Anointed One" would be "cut off" 483 years (69x7) after issuing the decree to restore and rebuild Jerusalem. This revelation from Gabriel clearly informed Daniel that the Messiah would be cut off from the land of the living and would die for the sins of man, thereby making atonement for us all. As predicted by God in these revelations to Daniel, it took seven "sevens" (or 49 years) to finish rebuilding Jerusalem and then another 62 "sevens" (or 434 more years) for a total of 483 years after the decree to rebuild Jerusalem was issued by King Artaxerxes (Ezra 7:1-13) before the Messiah or the Anointed One was to be cut off, once again pointing to redemption.

Throughout his lifetime—because of Daniel's earnest search for understanding—God continued to give visions with increasing detail about what was yet to come in regard to these kingdoms. On one of those occasions when continuing to reveal his plan for the nations to Daniel, the archangel Gabriel spoke frankly to him and then said, "Go your way because the words are closed up and sealed until the end" (Daniel 12:9). Even with all this revelation, there were still puzzles and mysteries yet to be revealed because the Messiah had not yet been crucified and redemption had not yet been fully accomplished.

Because of the details that Daniel records for each of the kingdoms and the incredible accuracy of these prophesies about each kingdom, some scholars believe that the book of Daniel must have been written after Jesus Christ died. However, Jesus himself testified to the authenticity of the book of Daniel as well as his life and his prophesies when he quoted him, stating, "So when you see standing in the holy place 'the abomination that causes desolation,' spoken of through the prophet Daniel—let the reader understand . . ." (Matthew 24:15).

Therefore, in a book written by Daniel and endorsed by Jesus Christ, prophecies of many kingdoms are revealed long before they ever happen. All of these prophesies and each of the kingdoms in their appointed time lead ultimately to the death of the Messiah or "the Anointed One being cut off." But that death becomes the pivotal point where now the eternal kingdom will begin to grow and fill the whole earth. God the Father uses both these revelations and the entire succession of kingdoms to once again point to redemption: the birth, life, death, and resurrection of Jesus Christ and what that would mean for all of us. Like the process of solving a Rubik's Cube, each kingdom has its time and place, and God's final outcome will only arrive if all these events unfold in the proper sequence or—as the Bible describes it—if they each happen in the "fullness of time." Yet another thread of the amazing tapestry that God has revealed throughout human history pointing all things in heaven and earth to the mystery of Godliness and the mystery of his kingdom.

"But in the days when the seventh angel is about to sound his trumpet, the mystery of God will be accomplished, just as he announced to his servants the prophets."

Revelation 10:7

7   **Collapsing Time**

Sustained Suspense

Our perception of time is so limited. We too quickly forget the past, and apart from God, we have no way of knowing the future. Even when we are intentional about looking back through time, we are far too often engaged in revisionist history. We are hardly able to keep up with the here and now of our lives, let alone attend to the larger timeline.

When I was a young boy in early elementary Sunday school hearing the stories of the children of Israel in the wilderness, I was pretty harsh on them and how poorly they kept up with their own timeline. I know, the Bible says that we are not supposed to judge each other, but it was so hard not to label them as dense idiots. I mean really! They had the *Shakina* presence of God in a pillar of fire by night and a pillar of cloud by day to go before them and lead the way. When they were being pursued by Pharaoh, they watched the Red Sea part, and they walked across on dry ground. Even more amazing was the way in which they saw the sea swallow up Pharaoh and his army, who would not stop trying to attack them. When they were thirsty, water came miraculously out of the rock. When they were hungry, manna and quail fell from heaven. Their shoes never wore out. The presence and glory of God were so overwhelming in their midst that Moses had to wear a covering over his face so that the "afterglow" of his visit with the great "I AM" would not blind the people. Even so, every time some new difficulty came along, the people grumbled that "they would have been better off left in Egypt rather than coming out here in the wilderness to die" (Exodus 14:12). It is at that point in the story that I often thought to myself, "How clueless and forgetful do you have to be to not acknowledge God's presence all around you?"

As I have gotten older and wiser, I have to acknowledge that I myself am sometimes that dense idiot. That is because over and over in my lifetime God has shown up and shown off. And yet when the next hurdle in life comes along, far too often I am caught up in the moment and forget to look back at all his blessings. In the timeline of

Collapsing Time

our own lives, we often forget too quickly that which is important to attend to.

Suppose for a little while I was able to look across time and collapse centuries of time into just a few moments—what would I find? If only briefly, I could see time from God's perspective and not mine, what might I discover? Cause and effect might take on a whole new meaning. The ripple effect of choices might become much more salient and clear. I might not be so quick to judge, and I might be much more thankful for the things he has accomplished in my life.

For example, collapsing 2000 years of time, I might realize that the only way that I could possibly be a Christ follower engaged in the process of writing this book would have to be directly related to the choices that 12 disciples made to follow Christ; to the choices that 120 followers made in an upper room on the day of Pentecost; and to the choices that 500 people made on the mount of ascension as Jesus went up into heaven. Somehow, across time, the choices that one of those—or more likely several of those—500 individuals made in their lifetime directly led to my accepting Jesus Christ as my savior nearly 2000 years later.

When we take that perspective, then it becomes obvious why God has said that "obedience is better than sacrifice" (I Samuel 15:22). I might sacrifice my time by going to church, my money by giving to missions, or my energy by being involved in some ministry effort. However, when God asks me to do something (no matter how small) if in the moment I end up not doing what he asks, what might the negative consequences be a thousand years from now should God delay his second coming? Who else's life might be affected? You see, we do not think that way, but God does. He sees the end from the beginning. He is not willing that any should perish, not even those who are in our distant future. We, on the other hand, far too often get all caught up in the busyness and clutter of the moment and lose that eternal perspective.

Perhaps I could use a couple of examples from my childhood to briefly focus on that different perspective. When I was a young boy in elementary school, I was involved in the Book of the Month Club. That does not mean that I got a new book and read it every month; it simply means that each month I received a paper that had several activities on it and the chance to purchase paperback books that were targeted for my age. Although my parents did occasionally buy a book or two for me, I enjoyed the activities as much as the chance to find a book I might like. One of the activities that I looked forward to each month involved an intricate line drawing that usually had about 10 to 12 items hidden somewhere in the drawing. The items I was supposed to find were drawn at the bottom of the page and then the goal was to find all of the items that were hidden somewhere in the larger drawing. I suppose you might call these puzzles an early form of "Where's Waldo." These are called pattern puzzles. The object or goal is to find a specific object in the complex—often repeated—patterns that make the finding more difficult. As you might have already guessed, I have always loved puzzles or some form of a challenge, so finding these objects was its own reward.

In the previous chapters we have seen how God hides pictures or types of redemption everywhere in his larger works of art called "Creation" and "Time." What is remarkable is that no matter how much clutter or busyness, no matter how many repeated patterns we might find at any point in time, if we are really looking, we are consistently able to find things that point to Jesus Christ and the process of redemption. In fact, one of the most famous sermons that I remember in my lifetime was Oral Roberts' sermon entitled "Who is that Fourth Man?" He later put that sermon in print in a book entitled *Christ in Every Book of the Bible.* As I have already stated several times now, God's plan was to bring everything in heaven and earth—both in his written Word and in all of creation—together to point to redemption: the birth, life, death, and resurrection of Jesus Christ and what it means for all of us. Because of this, it is easy to find Jesus Christ in every book of the Bible.

Another one of the activities or challenges that I enjoyed each month was the page that had a folded surprise drawing. You perhaps have seen these. It is an involved drawing with some theme. These drawings were usually very intricate. What was fascinating to me as a young boy was to try and figure out what I would be seeing once the paper was folded. The theme of the intricate drawing usually gave you all the clues you needed to figure it out. After examining the picture for a while, I would finally give in and fold the right side of the paper over to the left side where the dotted lines were indicated. Once folded, the two sides of the complex picture would be brought together to form a much simpler picture, which usually summarized the theme quite well. (See Figure 5 on page 79.)

Instructions for folding Figure 5

Fold the next page back once on the solid line on the right that runs from top to bottom. Then fold it forward once on the dotted line that runs from top to bottom of the page. Once folded correctly it should bring the two arrows together and the collapsed image will be revealed.

Fold the right section back on the solid line

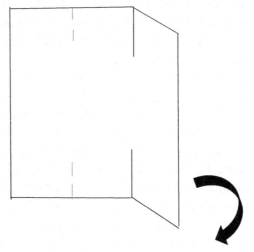

Down and behind the page

Then fold forward on the dotted line

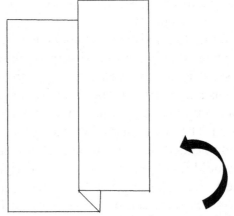

Up and over to the left till the two arrows touch

Figure 5. Folded Surprise Image
(See instructions on the previous page)

So what would happen if we collapsed time and also folded God's detailed drawing of history bringing the beginning of time closer to the end times? What clear simple picture might we see? In the Gospel of John, when addressing the beginning of time, he states the following:

> In the beginning was the Word, and the Word was with God, and the Word was God. He was with God in the beginning. Through him all things were made; without him nothing was made that has been made. In him was life, and that life was the light of men. The light shines in the darkness, but the darkness has not understood it. . . . The true light that gives light to every man was coming into the world. He was in the world, and though the world was made through him, the world did not recognize him. He came to that which was his own, but his own did not receive him. Yet to all who received him, to those who believed in his name, he gave the right to become children of God—children born not of natural descent, nor of human decision or a husband's will, but born of God. The Word became flesh and made his dwelling among us. We have seen his glory, the glory of the One and Only, who came from the Father, full of grace and truth. (John 1:1-14)

Before the world began, God had a plan. He already knew its outcome and was fully committed to its purpose, which is why he is able to say clear at the end of time, "Behold the Lamb of God, slain from the foundation of the earth" (Revelation 13:8). So near the very beginning of creation, when Satan thinks he has won in the Garden of Eden by tempting Adam and Eve to eat the fruit of the forbidden tree, God himself declares that this is only a minor irritant. He does so by saying that although Satan might strike the heel of Eve's offspring, that same offsping will crush Satan's head (Genesis 3:15). This is a prophecy that clearly looks ahead to the death and resurrection of Christ and what it will mean for us all.

Then John, the author of Revelation, was on the island of Patmos and had a vision about the end times. During part of that vision, he was overwhelmed that no one was found worthy to open the scrolls. "Then one of the elders said to me, 'Do not weep! See, the Lion of the tribe of Judah, the Root of David, has triumphed. He is able to open the scroll and its seven seals.' Then I saw a Lamb, looking as if it had been slain, standing at the center of the throne . . ." (Revelation 5:5-6).

So, clear at the end of time, we once again are pointed back to redemption; the birth, life, death, and resurrection of Jesus Christ, and what that means for us all. Even Jesus Christ says, "I am the Alpha and the Omega, the first and the last, the beginning and the end" (Revelation 22:13). He also stated that he is the one "who is, who was, and who is to come" (Revelation 1:8). This mystery of Godliness that throughout time continues to be revealed is a simple and clear message that everything is summed up in Jesus Christ. In fact, this mystery that we are to be stewards of will not be complete until the end of times. "But in the days when the seventh angel is about to sound his trumpet, the mystery of God will be accomplished, just as he announced to his servants the prophets (Revelation 10:7). So when we collapse time, the simple picture is redemption.

But what about all the busyness and clutter in the middle where we live? It is not just at the beginning of time and the end of time when God will make his plan clear. Not only did God use 1) people's lives as a process for foreshadowing the events of redemption, 2) the nation of Israel, and 3) an entire succession of kingdoms; he also used many events, religious ceremonies, and memorials to signify a type of foreshadowing of the birth, life, death, and resurrection of Christ. Redemption and what it means for us has been woven through every fiber of human history. Like another piece of a complex puzzle falling into place, God points us yet again to his focal point. And so we see— throughout the Old Testament and God's dealings with the nation of Israel—that their artifacts, religious ceremonies, sacrifices, and festivals would all be a symbol or "shadow" of redemption. Entire books have been written on the typology of Christ in the Old Testament. For brevity's sake, here are just a few of the symbolic archetypes of Jesus Christ and redemption.

- *Cities of Refuge*—Places of salvation where even though guilty of offense, a person could be redeemed and protected from the penalty that was justly deserved.
- *Noah's Ark*—A place of protection from the wrath of a holy God that was poured out on all mankind.

- *The Ark of the Covenant*—The ark contained the manna, which was life sustaining bread and a foreshadowing of Jesus who is "the bread of life"; it contained Aaron's staff, which represented God's sovereign choice of a mediator between God and man; and it contained the Ten Commandments, which was the moral law of God and which Jesus Christ would keep perfectly. It also shows how when God came down to man, he did so by descending on the mercy seat, which was sprinkled with blood by the high priest. This foreshadows the atoning blood of Jesus Christ, which forever covers the mercy seat and stands between the believer and the wrath of a holy God.

- *The Brazen Serpent*—Jesus states that "just as Moses lifted up the snake in the wilderness, so must the Son of Man must be lifted up" (John 3:14) so that all who look on him might be saved.

- *The Golden Candlestick*—Just as the golden candlestick was the light in the tabernacle, Jesus is "the light of the world." Also other than the mercy seat, which was the dwelling place for God the Father, the only other object in the temple that was made of pure gold was the candlestick. It also was not to be poured into a mold. Instead it was to be made of beaten gold just as Jesus Christ was beaten and bruised.

- *The Golden Altar*—An altar of incense that points to Christ our intercessor. Both in the Old and the New Testaments, incense was seen as the prayers of God's people and prayers come up to God's throne as a sweet smelling incense. After the resurrection, we learn that Jesus is our great high priest "who forever lives to make intercession for us" (Hebrews 7:25).

- *The Passover Lamb*—As a representation of the redemption that would come through the shedding of the blood of Jesus Christ there were many similarities in the sacrifice. The Passover sacrifice was selected on the tenth day of the month of Abib/Nisan in the same way that Jesus rode into Jerusalem to keep the Passover on the 10 day of Abib/Nisan. Afterward the Passover sacrifice was to be kept in the community for five days. So even though Jesus was being pursued by the priests for the purpose of killing him, he openly taught the community of Israel in the temple for the next five days. In preparation of the sacrifice, no bones were to be broken. In a similar manner, even though it was common for the Romans to beak the leg bones of someone being crucified to speed up the process of death, Jesus willing gave up his spirit and therefore the soldiers did not have to break his bones because he was already dead. When the lamb was slain for the Passover, the blood was placed upon the door posts on the threshold and on the lintel in the shape of a cross as a sign for the redemption of their firstborn male child. Jesus' blood on the cross was the sign of man's redemption from sin and death. In the Jewish ceremony hyssop was used to place the blood on the door posts and lintel. In the same way hyssop was used to give Jesus his last drink on the cross. The Passover lamb died so that the Israelites might live temporarily. Jesus died so that mankind might live eternally. The Passover sacrifice was the food of the sacred feast which they ate so they might live. In like manner Paul identifies Jesus as our Passover Lamb that we might observe the Eucarist by eating his flesh (the bread) and drinking his blood (the wine). As a meaningful and significant part of the Jewish covenant obligations, the first Passover and the Passover meal were to be remembered and partaken by every generation. In like manner, Jesus told his disciples and all those who would follow that every time you eat the bread and drink the wine "do this in remembrance of me" (Luke 22:19. And now for every generation until the Lord returns this holy sacrament is remembered. Since God had specifically told Moses how to prepare the Passover meal, he intentionally designed every detail to point forward to the passion of Jesus Christ, his death on the cross, and what it would mean for all mankind.

We could go on to talk about the Laver of Brass, the Mercy Seat, the Tabernacle, the Temple, the First Fruits, the Atonement Sacrifices, the Scapegoat, Peace Offerings, and the Sin Offering as well as many other religious ceremonies and festivals. While not all inclusive, this is the start of a good list of items that God uses in the Jewish culture to point forward to the Messiah.

So after all these clues to the mystery of Godliness are sprinkled throughout the ages past, the Messiah came and was born in a manger, astounded the people and the religious leaders, was crucified on a cross, was resurrected from the dead, and then ascended back to the Father in heaven. But the symbols of redemption have only just begun, for throughout the New Testament and to this day, we see many more pictures hidden everywhere in plain sight of the process of redemption—all pointing back to Jesus Christ.

- Every time a **salvation** occurs, we are reminded that there is salvation in no other name but Jesus.
- Each time there is a water **baptism**, it is a physical example of the old life dying and being buried with Christ and then rising to newness of life in Christ Jesus.
- Every time we take **communion**, we are reminded of redemption and Jesus Christ sacrificial death on our behalf. "Do this in remembrance of me" (Mark 14:22).
- Jesus Christ came to baptize with fire. The outpouring of the **Holy Spirit** was the culmination of Christ's work on earth. The goal of the Holy Spirit is always to point back to Jesus and bring all things to remembrance pertaining to him.
- The **cross** is the central symbol of the Christian religion and points to the crucifixion of Jesus Christ and the redeeming benefits of his passion and death.
- Each time someone is **healed**, we are reminded yet again that "by his stripes we are healed" (Isaiah 53:5).
- **Miracles** still happen. Because of the redemption provided by the birth, life, death, and resurrection of Jesus Christ, we are commissioned as his disciples to heal the sick, raise the dead, cleanse those who have leprosy, and drive out demons (Matthew 10:8).

Even from the foundations of the earth and clear till the end of times, the mystery of Godliness will continue to be in the process of being revealed. Sometimes we find that—just like the children of Israel—it is far too easy to lose sight of this in all the business and clutter of our times. If we are not careful, the cares of life too easily choke out our awareness, and even though the reminders and symbolic representations are everywhere, we may have trouble noticing them in all the repeated patterns of everyday living. Even so, the mystery still surrounds us everywhere and will not be fully accomplished until the seventh angel sounds his trumpet as revealed in the book of Revelation. In the meantime, God continues to point to his plan of redemption by using religious ceremonies, festivals, sacrifices, the design of his tabernacle, sacraments, salvations, water baptism, healings, the miraculous, the natural, and the supernatural. All of these throw clues flagrantly everywhere one might look in hopes that we will notice and choose to love him and be part of his plan.

"And he made known to us the mystery of his will according to his good pleasure, which he purposed in Christ, to be put into effect when the times will have reached their fulfillment—to bring all things in heaven and on earth together under one head, even Christ."

Ephesians 1:9-10

8	**The Master Designer**
	Mystery Maker

Creativity requires focus. Have you ever noticed how truly creative people have the ability to direct your focus to the center or the core of their creation? Great writers are able to say volumes in just a few key words strategically placed. Musicians keep bringing us back to the musical theme of their composition. Artists direct our attention to a central focal point in their work of art.

This is done through many different styles and mediums, but all skillful creations actively direct the viewer's attention. The writer accomplishes this through foreshadowing and other literary techniques; the musician does it through recurring themes, tempo, and dynamic; the poet does it through, meter and rhyme; the painter uses light, shadows, color, brush strokes, structure, and perspective all of which direct your attention to the main focus of their composition. Here are some famous examples:

- *Michelangelo's Sistine Chapel*—Even though there is an entire chapel full of his great paintings and artistic work, no matter where you look in the room, your attention cannot help but be drawn to the center of the ceiling where the hand of God and the hand of man meet in Michelangelo's most famous painting. Many of the characters of the Old Testament are depicted on the ceiling using small, tightly grouped figures to portray the story. However, when it comes to the *Creation of Adam*, the narratives have been paired down to depict only the essential figures on a monumental scale. Because of this difference, Michelangelo is able to convey a strong sense of emotion that can be perceived from the floor of the chapel, so your attention is drawn into this focal point. Additionally, he paints fictive columns on the side walls of the chapel as well as supporting figures that also draw your attention up to the ceiling where his primary focal point resides. Even on the ceiling as well, the architecture that already existed is enhanced by his paintings that make the architecture seem even more complex. So next to real columns and arches, Michelangelo has painted his fictive columns and arches. All of this serves to frame the nine larger panels he has painted in a manner to draw you even more significantly to his main focal point where God connects with man.

- *Leonardo DaVinci's Mona Lisa*—Although the smile in the painting is admittedly not the most beautiful or happiest of smiles, somehow it is still the world's most famous smile. This is so because of the many hours DaVinci spent trying to understand the anatomy of the face and in particular the muscles that control the movement of a smile. In recreating this knowledge on canvas, he used many different glazes that allow for varying degrees of light reflectivity, giving his paintings depth. He also used many extremely light, irregular brush strokes that make the tissues of the lips and cheeks seem to come alive. He also understood the science of optics and how the retina of your eye works. As a result, he used that knowledge to enhance the experience of the smile. If you look at it directly, you can see the slightly down-turned corners of her lips. But as you look away to other parts of the painting, her smile becomes more pronounced as you no longer attend to the downturn. Because this slight change in perception gives the impression that all of a sudden she is smiling more than she was a moment ago, you cannot help but have your attention arrested. This, in turn, once again draws you back to the world's most famous smile. Even though there is much more we could address in the painting of the *Mona Lisa*, all of DaVinci's efforts inevitably draw the viewer back to his focal point, which is her smile.

- How about a painter who is more recent, such as *Thomas Kinkade, the "Painter of Light"*—A term that he gave himself and protected by a trademark. Although some might argue about whether he is a master painter or should even be discussed in the same vein as Michelangelo or Leonardo DaVinci, he certainly was a prolific artist whose works were more widely distributed than many other current artists. In each of his paintings he used color and contrast to draw attention to some focal point. In most of his paintings, it is accomplished by using some source of light. Although he was an adeptly skilled artist whose talents included many genres, his

worldwide acclaim came mainly from his use of luminism—A painting style that emphasizes a unique clarity of light. For example, it might be the warm glow of a fireplace just inside the window of a quaint cottage on a cold winter's night or the warning beacon atop a stalwart light house on the edge of a craggy cliff above the choppy and stormy waves of an angry sea. His paintings would often use multiple sources of light to suggest the presence of people but without the actual figures present in the painting. As a result, this allows the viewer to imagine themselves in his pastoral settings. Whether you can see yourself in the setting he has chosen for a particular painting or not, whatever the source of light is, his paintings draw you in to that focal point.

- *Beethoven's Fifth Symphony,* Perhaps the quintessential four notes—One note repeated three times followed by a longer note a third of the scale down. This melody is played in a short-short-short-long rhythm. It was praised by critic E. T. A. Hoffman "as "one of the most important works of the time." Beethoven's short little motif comes again and again throughout the whole symphony. These four notes take on various characters as they migrate through the different sections of the orchestra and progress through the different movements of the piece. Sometimes foreboding, sometimes triumphant they continue to shift from different pitch centers to different dynamics all in a way that has had tremendous appeal well beyond the realm of classical music. Throughout his composition, Beethoven keeps bringing you back to this four-note theme, the focal point of his musical masterpiece that is perhaps more widely known than any other piece of classical music and is considered one of the cornerstones of western music.

In each instance, great works of art all direct attention to a central or critical focal point. How much more so does the Author of all creation direct our attention to one central and key focal point? In the Bible we read that everything in heaven and earth is brought together in one focus, one point in time and space, for one purpose (Ephesians 1:9-10). God has a plan, and everything will be brought into conformity with that plan. As we have already learned, God hides the clues to his plan everywhere in plain sight. Like a gigantic jigsaw puzzle, there are many, many pieces in the mystery of his plan. Although it is an extremely complex and intricate puzzle, God declares that he will fit all the pieces of the puzzle into a brilliant solution.

In the first chapter of Ephesians, God assures us that he has a plan and that he is working out every detail in heaven and on earth to conform to the purpose of that plan. Like a skilled craftsman, he intricately weaves the threads of his tapestry in ways that focus our attention on one thing. What is that focus? What is God's Plan?

According to Paul's writings "Beyond all question, the mystery of Godliness is great:

He appeared in a body,
  was vindicated by the Spirit,
  was seen by angels,
  was preached among the nations,
  was believed on in the world,
was taken up in glory"   (1 Timothy 3:16)

And so, as we have seen throughout our study so far, the mystery is the story of the birth, life, death, resurrection, and ascension of Jesus Christ and what that means for all those who recognize and accept him.

As stated in his word, "Through you, God has chosen to make known among the Gentiles the glorious riches of this mystery, which is Christ in you, the hope of glory" (Colossians1:27). God's focal point is redemption. If you ever want to fully understand God's plan, you must first discover how he is actively going about the business of conforming everything in heaven and earth into a process that points to the focal point of his master creation, which is redemption: the birth, life, death, resurrection, and ascension of Jesus Christ the Messiah and what it means for all mankind.

Make no mistake; this is no small task. As somewhat of a dabbling artist myself, I know how difficult it is to direct the focus of an audience toward a core issue. And that is true even when the raw materials are totally passive and compliant. Now imagine for a moment if your raw materials (paint, notes, and words) could talk back, had a mind of their own, and were constantly choosing to do their own thing instead of what you required. Only then do you begin to get a picture of the tremendous complexity of God the Father's (the Master Designer's) creative endeavor. He weaves every thread and fiber of time, space, men's lives, the succession of kingdoms and nations, the natural world, and the world of the supernatural into one glorious tapestry that points to redemption. He will do so with such skill that he is able to declare that men are without excuse because all of creation points to the nature of God and to redemption.

In fact, this majestic tapestry of redemption could be likened to a crossword puzzle. In a crossword puzzle all the necessary clues have already been provided. Each new word that is entered into the puzzle overlaps and intersects with other words in the puzzle. The placement of one word is predetermined by the way it intersects with those other words. Ultimately, to solve the crossword puzzle, you have to find out how each clue provided leads to a new word that interacts with the others already revealed.

In his master design, God has revealed all the necessary clues as we have seen already. Each life lived and each historical event that unfolds leads us inexorably to the story of redemption. The metaphorical symbols, the not-so-subtle foreshadowing, and even the direct prophecies are all intertwined. Amazingly, each piece of the tapestry is predetermined by its interaction with the other pieces of God's plan. In fact, Paul states that "For those God foreknew he also predestined to be conformed to the image of his Son, that he might be the firstborn among many brothers and sisters" (Romans 8:29). He also states that because of this plan of redemption, "he predestined us for adoption to sonship through Jesus Christ, in accordance with his pleasure and will" (Ephesians 1:5). God goes to extraordinary lengths to have everything in heaven and on earth bring us inevitably back to the birth, life, death, resurrection, and ascension of Jesus Christ and what that will mean for all mankind.

So God points to redemption through the prophets, through his Word (the Holy Bible), and through men's lives, which he directs as an archetype and shadow of his own. God points to redemption through events in history, through entire nations such as Israel, through the succession of kingdoms, and through genealogical records. He focuses on redemption through the sacraments of both the old covenant and the new. God powerfully focuses on redemption through the process of salvation in each of hundreds of thousands of human lives. He uses healing, miracles, the natural world, and the world of the supernatural. All point to the birth, life, death, and resurrection of Christ and what that means for individuals like you and me. Redemption is God's focal point.

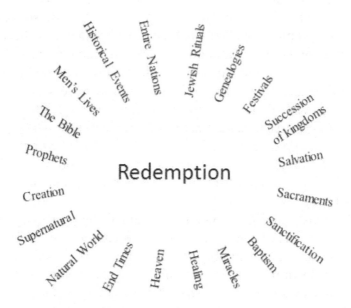

Figure 6: God's Focal Point

God works out every detail in heaven and on earth to conform to his plan. In the unfolding of his plan, we see that like the mechanical puzzle of the Oriental treasure box, all the clues are hidden in plain sight. Like the physical puzzle of the two beads which must spin out to opposite ends of the puzzle, answers are much easier to see than one might at first believe and are best revealed through a choice of active involvement. Like the jigsaw puzzle, through 39 other puzzles (the books of the Old Testament), he tells us his plan outright. As with the trivia puzzle, you will only see the connections between events and recognize the foreshadowing if you know all the details of the stories. Like the logic of the Sudoku puzzle, the placement of each event in history affects all the others. Like the combination puzzle of the Rubik's Cube, each part has its proper place and can be solved only if events unfold in the proper sequence. As with any visual puzzle, we see more clearly how simple and straight forward God's plan is when we collapse time. And finally, as we see here—like the linguistic focus of the crossword puzzle—all the necessary clues have already been provided through his Word, and they all intersect with each other so that no matter where we look in all of human history, we are pointed once again to redemption—the birth, life, death, and resurrection of Jesus Christ and what that means for all mankind.

"My purpose is that they may be encouraged in heart and united in love, so that they may have the full riches of complete understanding, in order that they may know the mystery of God, namely, Christ."

Colossians 1:25-27

9   **Redemption**

The Core Conundrum

And finally, we are brought to the greatest puzzle of all. How do you redeem the irredeemable? If you look up how to solve an unsolvable problem on YouTube, you will fairly quickly come across a video of a young man challenging others with what at first seems like an unsolvable problem. The goal of the puzzle is to connect three different houses with three different utilities without crossing any of the connecting lines. For example, each of the three houses needs to be connected to water, gas, and electricity. The challenge is that none of the utility lines can cross over each other. So, the limitations of the puzzle include the fact that you can only draw the connecting lines from each of the utilities to each of the houses on one single surface, yet all the homes have to be connected to all of the utilities, and none of the lines can cross each other.

If, as most people do, you attempt to solve this problem by drawing on one flat piece of paper, you will never be able to solve the puzzle. The only way to solve the problem, as revealed in the video, is to step out of the normal two-dimensional perspective and move to a three-dimensional surface such as a torus. In geometry, a torus is a surface of revolution generated by revolving a circle in three-dimensional space about an axis that is in the same plane with the circle. The easiest example of this shape would be the shape of a bagel. If the single surface you are drawing on is the surface of a bagel, then you are able to draw all three houses, all three utilities, and all three relevant connecting lines without crossing over any line. This is possible because some lines can travel horizontally, some lines can travel up or down around the outside of the bagel, and some lines can travel up or down around the inside of the bagel. Try it for yourself. You will find that it works beautifully. However, for this solution to work, the underlying assumptions about the nature of the single surface must be challenged. The puzzle solver must change their fundamental paradigm or way of thinking.

So it is with redemption. If it is at all possible, it will be so only if we as the human race challenge our fundamental assumptions about the nature of a potential relationship with God. By definition, "God is love" (1 John 4:8). But love, by its very nature, implies relationship. God said that it was not good for man to be alone (Genesis 2:18) and that we were created for relationship. We know that God longs for relationship with mankind (Proverbs 8:17), that he created us for his pleasure to be in relationship with him (Revelation 4:11), that he gave us a heart to know him (Jeremiah 24:7), and that he first loved us (1 John 4:19). He also said that all of the law and prophets are fulfilled in relationship (Matthew 22:40) and that he is not willing that any should perish but that all might be in relationship with him (2 Peter 3:9). All of this brings us to the core conundrum: how can a holy God have a relationship with a defiled people?

After all, "all have sinned and fallen short of the glory of God" (Romans 3:23). "There is no one righteous not even one" (Romans 3:10). Sin and iniquity have made a separation between man and God (Isaiah 59:2). "If we say we have no sin, we deceive ourselves, and the truth is not in us" (1 John 1:8). "For, all we like sheep have gone astray" (Isaiah 53:6). So "if we say we have not sinned, we make God a liar, and his word is not in us" (1 John 1:10).

All of this creates a dilemma for mankind because the Bible says that God "does not have pleasure in wickedness; neither will evil dwell with him" (Psalm 5:4). It also states that he "alone possesses immortality and dwells in unapproachable light, whom no man has seen or can see" (1 Timothy 6:16). Because God's holiness and perfect judgement requires that he must condemn sin if it fully enters his presence, we—in our fallen nature—full of sin are cut off from him.

Even so, we understand that God is omnipresent, that he is everywhere and in everything. As a result, we know—at least in part and especially for a Christian believer—that he is with us, he is in us, he is all around us, and that he loved us even while we were yet sinners (Romans 5:8). Still, this all relates to how he chooses to approach us. We, on the other hand, dare not approach God in his full glory and holiness. This was particularly true prior to Jesus Christ and his redemptive role. As a result, we see the prophet Isaiah in the presence of the Almighty say, "Woe is me, for I am undone; because I am a man of unclean lips, and I dwell in the midst of a people of unclean lips, and my eyes have seen the King, the Lord Almighty" (Isaiah 6:5-6). To be okay in that moment, one of the seraphim serving before the throne of God has to take a coal off the holy altar and touch his lips to take away Isaiah's guilt and atone for his sin. All of this occurs so that the prophet Isaiah can survive being in the presence of God Almighty—even when it is only in a vision.

Even after the redemptive work of Jesus Christ on the cross, John wrote that he saw a vision of the Lord "like the sun shining in all its brilliance . . . and fell at his feet as though dead" (Revelation 1:16-17). Once again the Lord has to reach out to John and say "fear not" for things to be okay. So even after the redemptive work of Christ when we can "boldly approach the throne of grace" (Hebrews 4:16), we had best do so with the fear of the Lord, with humility and with thankfulness for Jesus Christ's atoning work.

The Bible is clear that "the fear of God is the beginning of wisdom" (Psalm 111:10). We cannot even hope to approach a glorified and holy God on our own terms. In spite of this, human beings keep trying to put forth the idea that somehow we can make it on our own. Our contemporary society of tolerance and inclusion calls out saying that Christianity is too narrow and that it is too exclusive. They might even say that is politically incorrect. They also suggest that there are many paths to God. But God, through his Word, shows us that he has already given humankind every opportunity so that they cannot argue that they were not given a chance.

If we look across time in the Bible, we find that God has approached us on many different occasions and given mankind many opportunities to try to get it right on their own:

- *During the Age of Innocence*—God approached Adam and Eve in the Garden of Eden with a simple test to see if mankind could obey one simple directive: "You must not eat from the tree of the knowledge of good and evil (Genesis 2:17). Obviously they failed the test, and all of humanity plunged into sin at the "fall of man." As a result, God had to make coverings for Adam and Eve by the sacrifice of an animal and expel them from the garden because of their sin.

- *During the Age of Conscience*—from Adam to Noah, God tested us to find out what mankind might do when guided only by his or her own conscious. This is summed up when God talked to Cain saying, "If you do what is right, will you not be accepted?" (Genesis 4:7). As we all know from the story, Cain ended up killing his brother Abel, and once again mankind failed the test.

Again God had to intervene and create cities of refuge for offenders. Finally the wickedness became so great that God brought a flood to purge the sin and start over.

- *During the Age of Human Government*—From Noah to Abraham, God gave mankind a chance to follow human laws to see if they could live within that framework. Yet again mankind failed by gathering in the plain of Shinar, trying to build the Tower of Babel and attempting to reach to the heavens on their own, thus becoming independent of God (Genesis 11). In this instance, once again God had to intervene and confound their languages so that they would no longer be unified in their evil purpose.
- *During the Age of Promise and Covenant*—From Abraham to Moses, God tested one chosen group of people to see if they could live in covenant relationship with him. Will mankind keep a covenant with God? Part of the covenant involved promises that God would keep no matter what. But also in the covenant were conditions that the descendants of Abraham failed to keep. So a covenant of a Promised Land and a blessing with Abram ended up with his descendants in bondage and slavery in Egypt. As a result, the book of Genesis, which had started with the majestic words "In the beginning God created," actually closes out with the sad words "in a coffin in Egypt." So once again, God intervened and rescued a little baby boy in the bulrushes, a baby named Moses, who grew to become a deliverer of the Israelites.
- *During the Age of Law*—from Moses to Christ, God tested the nation of Israel to see if they would follow his ways if his precepts were spelled out in every minute detail. The Israelites promised that "all that the Lord has spoken we will do" (Exodus 19:8). Even so, the history of Israel is one of persistent violations of God's laws. Consequently, God once again intervened, and through the use of other nations, the Israelites were driven out of the Promised Land into captivity, first Israel and then Judah.

Over and over again God has given mankind different opportunities to see if we can get it right and live holy lives. He knew that mankind's principle argument would be that he never gave them a chance to do it on their own. So historically he gave us every imaginable kind of chance, and over and over again mankind has proven that on our own, we could not be holy. Even our contemporary society cannot live holy lives:

- We can protest all we want and say that Christianity is too narrow and limiting. And God would agree by saying that we should "enter by the narrow gate; for wide is the gate and broad is the way that leads to destruction (Matthew 7:13).
- The world asks, "Can't we all just get along?" And once again God will say that "light cannot have fellowship with darkness" (2 Corinthians 6:14). We should try to be redemptive. There is a process for that. But if a person continues to choose a path of sin, then we are to have nothing to do with them (Matthew 18:15-17).
- We can, as a society, protest that it is not politically correct to be so exclusionary. But once again God would say, "I have not come to bring peace but a sword. For I have come to set a man against his father, and a daughter against her mother, and a daughter-in-law against her mother-in-law. And a person's enemies will be those of his own household. Whoever loves father or mother more than me is not worthy of me, and whoever loves son or daughter more than me is not worthy of me" (Matthew 10:34-38).
- In our fallen state collectively as this world's population, we want to believe that there are many paths to God. But Jesus Christ himself said that "I am the way, the truth, and the life. No one comes to the Father except through me" (John 14:6).

Our failed attempts and God's unchanging nature can make this all seem overwhelming and hopeless because even though God is clearly not willing that any should perish, he is not willing to compromise on holiness and integrity either. This brings us back to the core conundrum: how do you redeem the irredeemable? Here is where God steps out of the perspective of the world and chooses to operate from a completely different paradigm. If the world is incapable of approaching a holy God, then God, himself, from another dimension will approach the fallen world. He does so through the birth, life, death, and resurrection of Jesus Christ. In doing so, he forever answers the question: "If it is so complicated and mankind cannot get it right, then why doesn't God just make it simple?" Well, he has done just that. He has made it simple, and he does make a way for the impossible. It is as simple as "For God so loved the world that he gave his only begotten son that whosoever believes on him shall be saved (John 3:16). If you believe, you will be saved. Unfortunately, we are a stubborn people; we do not want to accept the simple answer. So God took the time throughout human history to prove to us that the complex ones do not work. The good news is that if you are willing to abandon your own attempts at proving you are good enough and if you are willing to accept by faith that God changed the paradigm and already provided the answer for your shortcomings by sacrificing his Son Jesus Christ, then by faith the process of redemption can take effect in your own life. Then, once again, as in so many other lives throughout history, the impossible becomes possible. The irredeemable can by faith be redeemed.

Parables

God's Purpose

"Beyond all question, the mystery of godliness is great:

He appeared in a body,
   was vindicated by the Spirit,
      was seen by angels,
      was preached among the nations,
   was believed on in the world,
and was taken up in glory."

1 Timothy 3:16

10   The Mystery Revealed

A Perplexing Presence

There once was a stone that the builders rejected.

This is such a short, simple phrase. Even so, it is full of meaning and revelation. Like all parables, it involves a simple straight forward story designed to illustrate a much more involved moral concept or lesson. In this case, it is the culmination of all the puzzles we have been addressing. It is the arrival of the mystery long foretold. So finally, the mystery is revealed, the pieces of the puzzle fall into place, and the Messiah is born. Of him "in Scripture it says: See, I lay a stone in Zion, a chosen and precious cornerstone, and the one who trusts in him will never be put to shame. Now to you who believe, this stone is precious. But to those who do not believe, 'the stone the builders rejected has become the cornerstone' and 'a stone that causes people to stumble and a rock that makes them fall'" (1 Peter 2: 6-8).

God incarnate, both God and man, is now living, breathing, and moving on this small planet we call earth. To every believer this incarnation is precious. But to all others who would like to think that Jesus was just a good man, the mystery is not over, the puzzles are not all solved. For we come face to face with the Messiah and are presented with an awful dilemma. As C.S. Lewis explains in his book *Mere Christianity*, let us make no patronizing statements about Jesus Christ simply being a good man. He did not leave us that option. He himself declared that he is the Son of God. He challenged both his disciples and the religious leaders by stating that when he is killed, in three days he will rise again from the dead. According to C.S. Lewis, this puts him squarely in one of three camps (liar, lunatic, or Lord). If he knows this is not true but says it anyway, he is a liar. If he believes it to be true but in actuality it is not, then he is a lunatic, similar to someone who might believe they are a poached egg. He cannot simply be a good man or a great moral teacher if he is a liar or a lunatic. But, because of his lifestyle and his teachings, many of the other religions of this world and even most of the rest of the secular world are not willing to call him a liar or a lunatic. Therefore, the only alternative left is that he is who he says he is—the Son of the living God. If he truly is the Son of God, then we are presented with an overwhelming paradox.

This mystery—Jesus himself—comes as paradox incarnate. Every move of this Messiah runs directly counter to human reason and expectation. His life, his ministry, his sayings, and his very existence all represent an extremely challenging and perplexing presence.

- He was a brilliant scholar and teacher who—even though he was fully able to confound the religious leaders and teachers of the law when he was only 12 years old—still waited patiently another 18 years until the fullness of time when he was 30 years old to start his earthly ministry. Even at age 30 when his mother implored him to do something about the lack of wine at a wedding, he says "woman, why do you involve me? . . . My hour has not yet come" (John 2:4). Who does that? Who takes a great gift or talent and places it on a shelf on hold for some later date?
- Even though he is the God of the entire universe, he still somehow managed to live a very ordinary life on earth for 30 years. His life was so ordinary that his own brothers and the townspeople where he grew up found it almost impossible to believe that he was the Messiah, even in the face of overwhelming miraculous proofs.
- He was a Jew and a religious leader who verbally attacked the Jewish religious leaders.
- He was the Jewish Messiah, who came with strength and power to deliver but did nothing to deliver the Jews from the Romans.
- He was the Jewish King who placed God's dealings with the Jews on hold to usher in the time of the Gentiles.
- He had an eternity of ages past in heaven to communicate with his heavenly Father. He had 30 years on earth in his human form to continue that communication and prepare for his earthly ministry. Even so, he still somehow found it necessary to spend much—if not most—of his three years of ministry withdrawing from the crowd and from his disciples to communicate with his heavenly Father.
- Everything about his birth, life, death, and resurrection had been mapped out. He was predestined and foreordained from the foundations of the world to live a life that had already been

scripted down to the most intricate of details. Each of these details under the anointing of the Holy Spirit had been carefully recorded in the writings of the prophets, and yet, he was not bogged down by the past and what had been prophesied. Neither was he looking to the future, worried about when and how all the little prophesies were going to be fulfilled in his life. Instead, he—more than any other person in human history—was able to live in the moment, in the immediate here and now of life's circumstances, so much so that even on the way to important meetings or healing engagements, he still had time to be fully with those who needed him along the way. He was very present in the moment. He still is today.

From that time and even to this day, Jesus Christ's perplexing presence becomes the ultimate stumbling block for mankind. Satan could not figure out or discern his plan. The Jewish religious leaders of his day would not accept his message. The Jewish zealots did not understand his military passivity. The wise teachers and educators were impressed by his knowledge but were not able to comprehend the authority by which he spoke. Amid the Greek and Roman culture with many deities, other religions of the world could not accept him as the only way to God the Father. Those who were not born of the Spirit saw both the revelation of Jesus Christ as Messiah and the preaching of his kingdom as foolishness. Why? Because in their versions of religion "they pursued it not by faith, but as if it were by works. They stumbled over the stumbling stone" (Romans 9:32).

Jesus Christ was and still is the ultimate stumbling block, a perplexing presence that most people both then and now do not know how to handle. Therefore, Jesus Christ himself stated that "you must become like a little child to enter his kingdom" (Matthew 18:3). You must give up your preconceived notions of religion and your persistent entrenchment in the traditions of man. You must accept him in faith, believing like a little child does. This is because your pride (like that of Satan's), your religion (like that of the Jewish leaders), your militant passion (like that of the zealots), your wisdom (like that of the teacher and educators), your tolerance (like that of the Greek and Roman pantheists), and your fallen earthly nature (like those who have not yet embraced the kingdom) all keep you from seeing him for who he really is. He is the very real and present Son of the living God. He is the ultimate stumbling block—the chief cornerstone who is still being rejected by mankind today. Even so, this chief cornerstone has been elevated to the position where everything else in all of human history is now in the process of conforming to his image. Everything will focus on him and revolve around him. In fact, one day "every knee will bow, of those in heaven, and those on earth, and those under the earth, and every tongue will confess that Jesus Christ is Lord to the glory of God the Father" (Philippians 2:10-11).

Over the years, many other authors have addressed this issue of how a "chief cornerstone" can become a "stumbling block." What they all consistently address is that most buildings, besides circular ones, have multiple cornerstones. In fact, there is only one type of building in recorded history that has a "chief cornerstone" or "capstone" as some translations call it. That building is a pyramid. The first stone carved in the pyramid was the capstone. From that, all the angles would be determined for the rest of the structure. Unfortunately, from then on until it could be placed on the top of the structure it had to be placed out of the way or in some way navigated around. It became a stumbling block that seemed to be in the way. However, once the pyramid was near completion, that "chief cornerstone" would be placed at the top of the structure where finally all could see that the entire structure had its shape and was defined by its relationship to this "capstone."

As we have examined these puzzles, we have seen a consistent pattern and design woven into the very fabric of eternity. God is actively shifting every part of time and space, heaven and earth, men and angels, not to mention the extreme limits he places on himself in order to do so, all in order to point to redemption (the birth, life, death, resurrection, ascension, and what it means for us). This "chief cornerstone," the lamb slain from the foundation of the world, is the pattern by and through which all other things are created. Unfortunately, for far too many, he will remain a stumbling block until the end times as recorded in Revelation 10:7 when "the seventh angel is about to sound his trumpet, the mystery of God will be accomplished, just as he announced to his servants the prophets." Then, at that time, it will become obvious to all that he is the chief cornerstone when his heavenly Father places him at the top of the structure of all things.

So, what is the one question that we keep coming back to that humans inevitably ask? Why? Why does God go to all this trouble? Why create a mystery woven into every part of space and time? What is his purpose? Why go to such incredible lengths? Why such an overwhelmingly elaborate plan? Paul clarifies this by saying this is "in order that they may know the mystery of God, namely, Christ" (Colossians 2:2).

God the Father had said, "See I lay a stone in Zion, a tested stone, a precious cornerstone for a sure foundation" (Isaiah 28: 16). He had intentionally placed his Son in the middle of the Jewish nation and then focused everything on him. Since God himself has purposely tried to narrow the focus of all heaven and earth—not to mention all of time and human history on to Christ—let us do so as well. For a few minutes let us hear what Jesus Christ has to say about these matters. I will suggest, though, that if you are anything like the religious leaders and zealots from the past or if you are like many other non-believers and tolerance preachers in our contemporary world or if you simply find it hard to become like a little child and just soak this all in unfiltered, listening to what Jesus has to say may be difficult for you. Why? Because it is hard to hear what the Messiah has to say when you are so annoyed because you keep stumbling over him.

But let us suppose for a moment we can embrace His message without stumbling. So, what does he say? When Jesus Christ (who is the entire focus of God the Father) finally speaks what is his focus? When the central character of all time, all heaven and earth, and all things past and present finally does begin his earthly ministry, what does he talk about? The answer is clear. In fact, Matthew states that after he came out of the wilderness full of the Holy Spirit and power that, "He spoke all these things to the crowd in parables, He did not say anything to them without using a parable" (Matthew 13:34).

So, God the Father has everything point to Jesus Christ the Son. Then Jesus Christ has everything focused on parables. This begs the question: what is the focus of all the parables? In almost every instance, the parables start out by stating that "The kingdom of heaven is like" or they reference the kingdom.

It quickly becomes evident that Jesus Christ's entire focus was the kingdom of heaven. When he was introduced by John the Baptist, the Bible says, "In those days John the Baptist came, preaching in the desert of Judea and saying, 'Repent, for the kingdom of heaven is near'" (Matthew 3:1-2). After Jesus was baptized by John the Baptist and then came out of the wilderness, "From that time on Jesus began to preach, 'Repent, for the kingdom of heaven is at hand'" (Matthew 4:17). In his first sermon on the mount, he started by saying, "Blessed are the poor in spirit, for theirs is the kingdom of heaven" (Matthew 5:3). When Mark talks about the earthly ministry of Jesus Christ, he says it this way: "Jesus did not say anything to them without using a parable" (Mark 4:34), which, as we have seen, were all about the kingdom of heaven. When Jesus sent out his disciples two by two it states that, "These twelve Jesus sent out with the following instructions: 'Do not go among the Gentiles or enter any town of Samaritans. Go rather to the lost sheep of Israel. As you go, preach this message: The kingdom of heaven is near'" (Matthew 10:5-7). At another time, when Jesus had removed himself to a solitary place, "the people were looking for him, and when they came to where he was, they tried to keep him from leaving them. But he said, 'I must preach the good news of the kingdom of God to the other towns also, because that is why I was sent'" (Luke 4:42-43).

Later when he sent out the 72 followers to preach, he "appointed seventy-two others and sent them two by two ahead of him to every town and place where he was about to go" (Luke 10:1). He also instructed them, "When you enter a town and are welcomed, eat what is set before you. Heal the sick who are there and tell them, 'The kingdom of heaven is near you'" (Luke 10:8). Even after he was raised from the dead and "after his suffering, he showed himself to these men and gave many convincing proofs that he was alive. He appeared to them over the period of forty days and spoke about the kingdom of God" (Acts 1:3).

God the Father's plan was to have everything in heaven and on earth point to the Messiah: the birth, life, death, and resurrection of Jesus Christ. So, when Jesus finally arrived here on this small planet, he pointed everything to the kingdom of heaven. If you want to know the purpose of God's amazing plan for the ages, all you need to do is look at the life of Jesus Christ. Jesus boldly proclaimed that it is all about establishing a kingdom—a living, unshakable kingdom that will never end—a kingdom where God's will is done on earth just as it is in heaven. If you are able to hear this without stumbling over it, Jesus himself says, "Blessed is anyone who does not stumble on account of me" (Matthew 11:6).

Through many different puzzles, God the father has revealed the mystery of Godliness. So, this mystery that had been foretold and foreshadowed finally arrived and was revealed in the form of God's Son, Jesus Christ. Then this amazing and perplexing presence, this chief cornerstone, this stumbling block with every fiber of his being and every ounce of his life set about the process of revealing the mystery of the kingdom of heaven. Even more amazing he invites us to be part of that kingdom.

"He told them, 'The secret of the Kingdom of God has been given to you. But to those on the outside, everything is said in parables so that, they may be ever seeing but never perceiving, and ever hearing but not understanding; otherwise, they might turn and be forgiven.'"

Mark 4:11-12

11	**The Sermons of Christ**

Baffling Sagas

There once was a magnet that attracted and repelled people.

As part of his plan, God had focused everything in heaven and earth on redemption. So now the mystery of God had been revealed in Jesus Christ the incarnate living and breathing Son of God. He walked among mankind uniquely both as a man and as God, the ultimate mystery in the flesh. Then for the few short years that he was on this planet, Jesus focused every part of his life and ministry on explaining how the establishment of the kingdom of heaven is the purpose for God's incredibly intricate and all-encompassing plan. His entire ministry here on earth was designed to reveal the mystery of God's kingdom. But despite how masterfully Jesus was revealing the kingdom, mysteries, hidden secrets, and treasures of eternity; they remained confounding to the world. Sometimes even his disciples failed to understand these kingdom principles in spite of the fact that Jesus went out of his way to explain them to his immediate followers. Even so, you have been given a promise that "the secrets of the kingdom of heaven have been given for you to know" (John 13:11). If you want to be part of that kingdom, the sermons of Christ will draw you in. But for others who do not choose to be actively involved in the kingdom, they will not perceive them, they will not understand them, and the sermons will push them away.

In revealing the mystery of the kingdom, Jesus preached many kinds of sermons with a variety of effects. There was . . .

- the sermon on the mount,
- the parables by the sea,
- sermons to his disciples about how to go out into the world,
- sermons about being either with God or with Satan,
- sermons full of woes unto religious leaders,
- sermons about the traditions of men,
- sermons that serve as warnings,
- sermons on the second coming,

- sermons on how to live after he goes back to heaven,
- and sermons on the end times as well as many others.

In all of these, Jesus communicated strange messages that were challenging to understand; baffling sagas that both at times compelled the people to follow him and at other times drove them away. He spoke messages that had never been heard before. Although he spoke with authority, he said confusing things like these:

- "The meek will inherit the earth" (Matthew 5:5).
- "Blessed are those who are persecuted" (Matthew 5:10).
- "You should love your enemies" (Matthew 5:44).
- "Blessed are you when people hate you" (Luke 6:22).
- "I am the bread of life" (John 6:48).

Jesus was constantly saying things so that even if the people heard it, they were not likely to understand. This is because he was in the process of revealing the kingdom of heaven in a way that only those earnestly seeking the things of God could comprehend. In fact, he specifically stated that he spoke this way so that "hearing they will not hear and seeing they will not see" (Luke 8:10). Only those diligently seeking the kingdom would understand it. Just as he had stated to the children of Israel, "you will seek me and you will find me when you search with all your heart" (Jeremiah 29:13), so also the kingdom of God would be found only by those who were searching with all their heart. He was clearly communicating that the kingdom was not one that could ever be embraced by the casual observer or the somewhat interested.

This different way of speaking—as well as the miracles—drew the crowds to him. In fact, "a great crowd of people followed Him because they saw the signs he had performed by healing the sick" (John 6:2). They marveled at the authority with which he spoke. But because so many were following him only for the miracles, he said even more difficult things that would then drive them away. For example,

- "Unless you eat my flesh and drink my blood, you will have no life in you. Whoever eats my flesh and drinks my blood has eternal life" (John 6:53-54).

- "Do not suppose that I have come to bring peace to the earth. I did not come to bring peace but a sword. I have come to turn a man against his father, a daughter against her mother-in-law; a man's enemies will be the members of his own household." (Matthew 10:34).
- "You will be hated by everyone because of me" (Matthew 10:22).
- "If your eye causes you to stumble, gouge it out and throw it away" (Matthew 18:9).
- "If anyone comes to me and does not hate father and mother, wife and children, brothers and sisters—yes even their own life—such a person cannot be my disciple" (Luke 14:26).
- "Let the dead bury the dead" (Matthew 8:22; Luke 9:60).

These strange and powerful sermons, full of authority, ended up driving away many of the initial followers. In fact, after Jesus had miraculously fed the multitudes, he challenged those followers by saying, "I tell you, you are looking for me, not because you saw the signs I performed but because you ate the loaves and had your fill" (John 6:26). They were seeking free food and not spiritual growth. They wanted healing, deliverance, and food rather than the healer, the deliverer, or the bread of life. He challenged them not to look for food that spoils but for food that endures to eternal life. He was very pointedly asking them to embrace the kingdom and not just the miracles. Unfortunately, many in the crowd were attracted to the material aspect of the signs that Jesus was performing rather than understanding their spiritual significance. In revealing the nature of the kingdom of heaven, Jesus was clearly communicating that it would not be a magical kingdom where everyone's material needs would be met. It was not to be a kingdom where God would be on tap for whatever we wanted. Even though miracles and the supernatural are part of the kingdom, they are to be signs that follow the believer and not the focus of the believer (Mark 16:17). So, through these sermons we also learn that this would be a kingdom that cannot be embraced by those who are only looking for material gain, the miraculous, or the supernatural.

Jesus' sermons also rocked the religious establishment. Although the religious leaders thought that they were well positioned in their traditions, their practices, and even in the things of God, he directly challenged their authority by saying things like these:

- "Woe to you teachers of the law and Pharisees, you hypocrites! You shut the door of heaven in people's faces" (Matthew 23:13).
- "Woe to you teachers of the law and Pharisees, you hypocrites! You travel over land and sea to win over a single convert, and when you have succeeded, you make them twice as much a child of hell as you are" (Matthew 23:15).
- "Woe to you, blind guides! . . . You blind fools! . . . You blind men!" (Matthew 23:16-19).
- "Woe to you teachers of the law and Pharisees, you hypocrites! You give a tenth of your spices—mint, dill, and cumin. But you have neglected the more important matters of the law—justice, mercy, and faithfulness" (Matthew 23:23).
- "Woe to you teachers of the law and Pharisees, you hypocrites! You clean the outside of the cup and dish, but inside they are full of greed and self-indulgence" (Matthew 23:25).
- "Woe to you teachers of the law and Pharisees, you hypocrites! You are like whitewashed tombs, which look beautiful on the outside but on the inside are full of the bones of the dead and everything unclean" (Matthew 23:27).
- "You snakes! You brood of vipers! How will you escape being condemned to hell?" (Matthew 23:33).

These are all part of amazing sermons full of statements that will either draw you in or push you away. Obviously, he was not making very many friends in religious leadership circles. He was, however, trying to reveal that the kingdom can never be embraced by those who are seeking power, position, significance, or earthly authority. Therefore, he often preached that we should humble ourselves, that the meek would inherit the earth, and that the last shall be first. Just as a magnet's strong positive end will attract the negative end of another magnet, the sermons of the strong Son of God will always attract the humble and meek of heart. In fact, in the sermon on the mount, Jesus had said "blessed are the poor in spirit for theirs is the kingdom of heaven" (Matthew 5:3). Essentially, he was saying that those who recognize that in themselves they are insufficient and lacking in the things of the spirit will be easily drawn to the all-sufficient Christ and his kingdom. On the other hand, just like a magnet's strong positive end will repel another magnet's positive end, those who position themselves as self-sufficient and as having power and status will be repelled by the idea of submission to a greater authority.

Jesus was in the process of revealing that power, authority, and significance belong to our heavenly Father in this new kingdom. His woes to the religious leaders at times seemed very harsh. And yet with each warning, criticism, or woe; he was revealing an important principle in the mystery of the kingdom of heaven. Yes, most definitely the kingdom of heaven was at hand, but it also was not accessible for those who selfishly continued to walk according to the world's principles and ideas. The kingdom of heaven would be a place where God's will is done on earth just as it is in heaven.

"O my people, hear my teaching; listen to the words of my mouth. I will open my mouth in parables, I will utter hidden things, things from of old."

Psalm 78:1-2

There once was a road map that did not match any earthly terrain.

For centuries God the Father had been revealing in a million different ways the mystery of godliness. And now Jesus Christ—the physical embodiment of that mystery—in a million different ways is revealing the mystery of the kingdom. Just as God the Father had used puzzles, riddles, and mysterious revelations to throw clues to us from every direction, now the Son of God was communicating in his own cryptic form to humans. In fact, "Jesus spoke all these things to the crowd in parables; he did not say anything to them without using a parable. So was fulfilled what was spoken through the prophet: 'I will open my mouth in parables, I will utter things hidden since the creation of the world.'" (Matthew 13:34-35).

Years earlier king Solomon—who, according to the Bible, was the wisest man who ever lived—had said, "Let the wise listen and add to their learning, and let the discerning get guidance—for understanding proverbs and parables, the sayings and riddles of the wise. The fear of the Lord is the beginning of knowledge" (Proverbs1:5-7). Wisdom and understanding come from having a healthy reverence and respect for the things of God and for the Almighty Creator. Just as in the past, when only those longing to understand the things of God would be able to understand his mysteries, so too now only those longing to be part of the kingdom would be able to understand the message of Jesus Christ. He warned the rulers of his day that those who relied on their own wisdom would only see this as foolishness. However, for those who would become like little children rediscovering their sense of humility and curiosity, the mysteries of the kingdom of God would be revealed. So, for the general public, "He did not say anything to them without using a parable. But when he was alone with his own disciples, he explained everything" (Mark 4:34).

He went on to explain that the kingdom is within you. In other words, by the power of the Holy Spirit that is alive in you once you become "born again," you are able to live in such a manner as to bring the kingdom of heaven to earth. But what does that kingdom life look like? It can be very difficult to wrap our heads around when it is so different from the everyday lives we see in our fallen world. They say a picture is worth a thousand words. So where do we find an effective picture of kingdom living? During his earthly ministry Jesus proactively lived out a brilliant picture for us. He is our perfect example. But he goes beyond just living the picture for us. Through the parables he very carefully explains the concepts and principles behind that kind of lifestyle. Under the direction of his heavenly Father and through the anointing of the Holy Spirit he reveals to us the keys to kingdom living and how to get on board with the Father's plan. This is so that God's will can be done in your life just as it is in heaven.

For three years, Jesus—speaking through parable after parable— taught us what the kingdom would look like in our lives and in our hearts. Each of his parables was complex and rich in meaning. In fact, many pastors over the years have preached an entire series of sermons on just one of these rich metaphors for the kingdom life. However, to get the impact and message of all the parables together, we can boil each of them down to their central message. So, if you long to be part of that kingdom—not just someday in the future but here in your lives right now—let us examine the various groups of parables and teachings and what they suggest for who we should be as the children of God. If the kingdom of God is "at hand," present in the here and now, and if it is "within us," what does it look like? What does the road map for living a Christian life look like?

The Parables of Jesus Christ

Creation   *What the Kingdom Is Like in Our Hearts*
and Nature

- The Seed Growing Is Inevitable (Mark 4:26-29) *If you scatter seed, it will grow, even if you do not know how it does.*
- The Sower and the Seeds (Matthew 13:3-9; Mark 4:3-9; Luke 8:5-8) *It hears the word, accepts it, and produces a crop.*
- The Weeds and the Wheat (Matthew 13:24-30) *It thrives even in the midst of weeds.*
- The Mustard Seed (Matthew 13:31; Mark 4:30-32; Luke 13:18) *It starts small and grows within us.*

118

- The Budding Fig Tree (Matthew 24:32; Mark 13:28; Luke 21:19-31) *It is filled with clues and signs if you look.*
- The Leaven (Matthew 13:33; Luke 13:20) *It will work its way into everything.*
- The Birds of the Air (Matthew 6:26; Luke 12:24) *It does not need to worry.*
- The Kernel of Wheat (John 12:24) *It is self-sacrificing.*
- Separating Good and Bad Fish (Matthew 13:47-50) *It is about identifying what is good.*
- The Flowers of the Field (Matthew 6:28-30; Luke 12:27) *It seeks first the things of God and is assured.*
- The Tree and Its Fruits (Matthew 7:16; Luke 6:43-49) *It is recognized by its fruit.*
- The Barren Fig Tree (Luke 13:6-9) *It must bear fruit or be cut down.*
- The Vultures (Matthew 24:28; Luke 17:37) *It is not led astray or deceived.*
- The Weather Signs (Matthew 26:2; Mark 8:11-13; Luke 12:54-56) *It knows how to interpret/discern the times.*

Light and Treasure　　　*What the Kingdom Is Like in Our Hearts*

- The Lamp (Matthew 5:14-16; Mark 4:21; Luke 8:16, 11:31) *It illuminates the darkness in our lives, so we do not stumble.*
- The Body's Lamp (Matthew 6:22; Luke 11:34-36) *It sees clearly and does not filter God and others through personal bias.*
- Salt of the Earth (Matthew 5:13; Mark 9:50; Luke 14:34) *It penetrates, purifies, and preserves.*
- New Wineskins (Matthew 9:16; Mark 2:21; Luke 5:36-39) *It does not hold rigidly onto the past but embraces change.*
- The Wise and Foolish Builders (Matthew 7:24-27; Luke 6:47-49) *It builds upon a sure foundation.*
- The Rich Fool (Luke 12:16-21) *It understands where real treasure lies.*
- The Hidden Treasure (Matthew 13:44) *It asks us to give everything.*
- The Pearl of Great Price (Matthew 13:45) *It recognizes God's worth.*

Service and Servanthood *What the Kingdom Is Like in Our Hearts*

- A Master and His Servants (Luke 17:7-10) *It recognizes God owes us nothing, we are his servants.*
- The Faithful and Unfaithful Servants (Matt. 24:45-51; Luke 12:42-46) *It serves with integrity and does not become lax.*
- The Ready Servants (Mark 13:33-37; Luke 12:35-38) *It waits with joyful anticipation for the master.*
- The Laborers in the Vineyard (Matthew 20:1-16) *It does not begrudge God his generosity.*
- The Talents (Matthew 25:14-30; Luke 19:12-27) *It puts God's gifts to work and produces.*
- The Dishonest Steward (Luke 16:1-12) *It is shrewd and makes good use of time and resources.*
- The Unmerciful Servant (Matthew 18:23-35) *It embraces forgiveness.*
- The Defendant (Matthew 5:25; Luke 12:58) *It embraces reconciliation.*
- The Householder's Treasure (Matthew 13:52) *It is balanced between law and grace.*
- The Vinedressers (Matthew 21:33-41; Mark 12:1-9; Luke 20:9-16) *It is not wicked but gives God his due.*
- The Two Debtors (Luke 7:41-43) *It builds great love by great forgiveness.*

Preparation and Vigilance *What the Kingdom Is Like in Our Hearts*

- The Unwilling Guests (Matthew 22:1-10; Luke 14:16-24) *It does not place self-interest above God's invitation.*
- The Marketplace Children (Matthew 11:16-19; Luke 7:31-35) *It recognizes that we must approach God on his terms and not ours.*
- The Lower Seat (Luke 14:7-11) *It seeks the place of humility.*
- The Bridegroom's Friend (John 3:28) *It eagerly waits on God.*
- Building a Tower (Luke 14:28-32) *It counts the cost.*
- The Bridegroom's Guests (Matthew 9:15; Mark 2:18; Luke 5:34) *It rejoices while he is near.*
- The Ten Virgins (Matthew 25:1-13) *It stays prepared and vigilant.*

- The Wedding Garment (Matthew 22:11-14) *It demands that we come prepared.*

Focus and   *What the Kingdom Is Like in Our Hearts*
Faithfulness

- The Unoccupied House (Matthew 12:43-45; Luke 11:24-26) *It realizes there is no deliverance from anything without dedication to something stronger.*
- The Strong Man Bound (Matthew 12:29; Mark 3:27; Luke 11:2.) *It does not become bound or entangled.*
- The Closed Door (Luke 13:24-30) *It walks the narrow path.*
- The Doorkeeper (Matthew 24:42; Mark 13:33-37) *It is vigilant.*
- The Thief in the Night (Matthew 24:42-51; Luke 12:32-48) *It guards what has been entrusted to it.*
- The Unjust Judge (Luke 18:1-8) *It is persistent and tenacious.*
- The Importunate Neighbor (Luke 11:5-8) *It recognizes God's willingness to give.*
- The Son's Request (Matthew 7:9-11; Luke 11:11-13) *It recognizes our kinship to God.*
- The Pharisee and the Publican (Luke 18:9-14) *It is humble and contrite.*
- The Divided Realm (Mark 3:24-26; Luke 11:17-20) *It stands unified.*

Redemption and   *What the Kingdom Is Like in Our Hearts*
Reconciliation

- The Sons (Matthew 21:28-32; John 3:35; John 5:19-20) *It does the will of the Father.*
- The Good Samaritan (Luke 10:25-37) *It reaches out to those who are different.*
- The Prodigal Son (Luke 15:11-32) *It rejoices in reconciliation.*
- The Lost Coin (Luke 15:8-10) *It spends all of its energy recovering the lost.*
- The Lost Sheep (Matthew 28:12-14; Luke 15:4-7) *It is active in seeking the lost.*
- The Gatekeeper's Voice (John 10:1-18) *It listens to God's voice and is not deceived by others.*

- The Doctor and the Sick (Matthew 9:12; Mark 2:17; Luke 5: 31) *It embraces the "sick" rather than the "well."*
- The Sheep and the Goats (Matthew 25:31-46) *It feeds, clothes, and shelters the widows and orphans.*
- The Rich Man and Lazarus (Luke 16:19-31) *It provides Justice.*

Through each of these parables, Jesus was teaching us what the kingdom life looks like in our hearts and, therefore, what our behavior should be. He was communicating clearly to us that the kingdom is not far away, but that it is immediate and at hand. This, however, could only be true to the extent that we—through the power of the Holy Spirit—take on the attributes and nature of this same Jesus Christ who was sharing these principles with us. Elsewhere, the apostle Paul talked about this as "being transformed and growing from glory to glory into the image of Christ" (2 Corinthians 3:18).

Jesus told the disciples that one of the roles of the Holy Spirit would be to bring to their remembrance all these things that he had taught them. To fully embrace the richness of what Jesus shared about this kingdom—which is at hand—it helps to approach these parables from multiple perspectives. As we have just done, it is very beneficial to get a bird's eye view by thoroughly reviewing all the main themes of each of these insightful parables. Having done so, it is also important to dive deeply into each parable to understand more of the details and impact of their lessons individually. That is where the previously mentioned series of sermons all on one parable can become very useful. Even so—while taking on the kingdom lifestyle often involves improving in one area or another at any given time—it remains important to see the big picture by reviewing them all.

Ultimately the parables that Jesus taught can only be useful to the degree that we apply their lessons in our lives. For those who are willing to see and for those who are ready to hear; the parables make the life instruction more straightforward, the material clearer to understand, and the insight easier to apply. For those who are either willfully or negligently disregarding the parables they become more difficult to understand and more obscure. That is why Paul talked about the message of the cross being foolishness to those who are perishing and spiritually dead (1 Corinthians 1:18). Even for those who are not spiritually dead and who have been born into the kingdom, neglect of these life lessons can make the kingdom of heaven harder to perceive in the here and now of our everyday lives.

However, when we listen to how Jesus explains the parables to his disciples, then we can learn powerful lessons for how to live in this alternative kingdom, the kingdom of heaven. As we then choose to live out the principles communicated, we become transformed. Each of these parables individually is one more cryptic clue showing us what that transformation looks like in our lives so that the mystery of the kingdom of God can be lived out every day in our own personal lives. Collectively the parables give us a very comprehensive picture of what it looks like to live a kingdom life. In effect, the parables are a road map to what the kingdom of heaven should look like within us.

"I have become its servant by the commission God gave me to present to you the word of God in its fullness—the mystery that has been kept hidden for ages and generations but is now disclosed to the saints."

Colossians 1:25-26

13   The Disciples Focus

Emboldened Enigmas

There once was an orphan who grew up to change the world.

The Gospel, the good news, the word of God in its fullness, this mystery that had been kept hidden for ages and generations was fully disclosed to the saints through the life and teachings of Jesus Christ. For three epic and eventful years, Jesus shared the principles of the kingdom of heaven, making them practical, straight forward, and simple. So, when Jesus the Messiah ascended into heaven, the disciples were finally ready to run with what they had learned during that time. And run they do.

Although spiritually each of them was no more than an impoverished orphan, God had sent his Son to die on a cross so that they each might receive adoption to sonship (Galatians 4:4-5). They had been "born" into the kingdom. So now as part of the "family" of God, the mystery of the kingdom was fleshed out in each of the disciples' experiences. They had tarried in the upper room, were filled with the Holy Spirit, and now they as well as all those around them were able to demonstrate the kingdom being truly at hand in their own lives. So much so, that miracles, salvations, transformations of lives, and even greater things than Jesus Christ had done were everyday occurrences for them.

Peter, an unlearned fisherman, preached a powerful sermon, and 3000 people were saved that day. Peter and John walked up to the gate called "Beautiful" as a lame man was asking for alms. Peter said, "Silver or gold I do not have, but what I do have I give you. In the name of Jesus Christ of Nazareth, walk" (Acts 3:6). As a result, the lame man immediately was healed. Even with just Peter's shadow falling on people, they were instantly healed (Acts 5:15).

Philip delivered the good news of the gospel to an Ethiopian and then was suddenly and miraculously transported to a city called Azotus (Acts 8:26-40). Stephen, even while he was being stoned to death, was able to give praise and thanksgiving to God and to ask for those who were stoning him to be forgiven (Acts 7:59-60). Paul, who was persecuting early believers, became one of the new converts and did many mighty exploits for God. Even while imprisoned for their faith, the early disciples sang praises unto God just before the prison's doors were shaken open, the prisoners were miraculously released from their bondage. These and many other remarkable miracles happened because the kingdom of heaven was not far off but was at hand in each of the disciples' lives.

As amazing as the miracles were, that was not the focus of the disciples. In fact, Jesus had said "these signs will accompany those who believe: in my name they will drive out demons, they will speak in new tongues, they will pick up snakes with their hands; and when they drink deadly poison, it will not hurt them at all; they will place their hands on sick people, and they will get well" (Mark 16:17-18). This was merely a byproduct of the disciples' focus. We read in the book of Matthew that Jesus had said if you "seek first the kingdom of God, and His righteousness; then all these other things shall be added unto you" (Matthew 6:33).

That was the disciples' secret. They had tapped into the mystery of God's kingdom, and by pursuing it, they were experiencing the same miraculous kind of journey through life that followed Jesus Christ everywhere he went. The kingdom was at hand—so much so that everyone around them sat up and took notice. This was particularly true for the elders and the teachers of the law in Jerusalem. "Annas the high priest was there, and so were Caiaphas, John, Alexander, and others of the high priest's family" (Acts 4:6). They felt threatened by the disciples' new powers. So, they had Peter and John forcefully brought before the Sanhedrin.

Then Peter filled with the Holy Spirit, said to them, "Rulers and elders of the people! If we are being called to account today for an act of kindness shown to a man who was lame and are being asked how he was healed, then know this, you and all the people of Israel: It is by the name of Jesus Christ of Nazareth, whom you crucified but whom God raised from the dead, that this man stands before you healed. Jesus is 'the stone you builders rejected, which has become the cornerstone.' Salvation is found in no one else, for there is no other name under heaven given to mankind by which we must be saved." When they saw the courage of Peter and John and realized that they were unschooled, ordinary men, they were astonished, and they took note that these men had been with Jesus. (Acts 4:8-13).

Paul in writing to the Romans said, "I am not ashamed of the gospel, because it is the power of God that brings salvation to everyone who believes: first to the Jew, then to the Gentile" (Romans 1:16). The disciples and apostles had developed a holy boldness. They were emboldened to proclaim Christ and his kingdom without fear or shame despite an oppressive Roman government or a jealous and corrupt religious leadership that tried to stop them. These early Christians were emboldened enigmas who demonstrated puzzling, mysterious, and almost inexplicable behavior.

I say "almost inexplicable behavior," but it can be explained. Jesus Christ had very carefully done so for three years as he preached "the kingdom of heaven is at hand." Through all kinds of parables, through personal lifestyle and self-sacrificing behavior, Jesus had methodically demonstrated what it meant to live this alternative kingdom life. Then he sent out his disciples by twos. "These twelve Jesus sent out with the following instructions: 'Do not go among the Gentiles or enter any town of the Samaritans. Go rather to the lost sheep of Israel. As you go, preach this message: The kingdom of heaven is at hand'" (Matthew 10:5-7). Later, when he sent out the 72 disciples to a broader audience, including the Samaritans, he said, "When you enter a town and are welcomed, eat what is set before you. Heal the sick who are there and tell them, 'The kingdom of God is near you'" (Luke 10:8-9). So, on multiple occasions, the disciples had been sent to preach that the kingdom of heaven was at hand. That was their commission by Christ, and they had been doing so.

Even so, initially they still did not fully understand all they had been told by Jesus concerning the kingdom. But after the day of Pentecost when they were all filled with the Holy Ghost with the evidence of speaking in tongues, it was a completely different story. Jesus himself had told them that one of the roles of the Holy Spirit would be to help bring to their remembrance all that they had been told concerning the kingdom (John 14:26). One of those things he had said was, "my food is to do the will of the father" (John 4:34). He also taught them to pray, "Thy kingdom come, thy will be done, on earth as it is in heaven" (Matthew 6:10). In seeking first the kingdom of heaven, they had learned to do the will of the father just as Jesus had done, and this new behavior was turning the known world upside down. They were doing God's will and living God's way by following God's words as laid out in the parables and as revealed to them by the power of the Holy Spirit.

A former pastor of mine, Rev. H. A. Brummett, used to have a carved wooden plaque in his office that stated, "The will of God; nothing more, nothing less, and nothing else." It is an exceptionally good motto for life. It was one that the disciples had learned to live out as they sought the kingdom of heaven first and lived out its principles. Through the power of the Holy Spirit, they were able not only to remember the lessons of the parables but also to live them out. Jesus had also told them that "my sheep know my voice." They had learned to listen to the voice of their shepherd—Jesus Christ. Now though the power of the Holy Spirit, they could listen as he helped them navigate the kingdom life. As such they were actively involved as ambassadors of the kingdom; they were emboldened enigmas, proclaiming the good news of the gospel, "which is Christ in you, the hope of glory" (Colossians 1:27).

As a young student at Oral Roberts University, I very well remember Oral Roberts' commission by God to "Raise up your students to hear my voice." Hearing the voice of God is absolutely essential if one is ever going to be able to "seek first the kingdom of God" (Matthew 6:33). Since the kingdom is a place where God's will is done on earth as it is in heaven, one definitely has to be able to hear from God in order to do his will. Both through his written Word—the Bible—and through the power of the Holy Spirit we are enabled to hear the voice of God in our day and time. As a result, when that indwelling of the Holy Spirit happens, when your primary focus is seeking first the kingdom, and when you as a result live out the meaning of the parables that Jesus has taught, then truly the kingdom is at hand and comes alive on earth just as it is in heaven.

John the Baptist's focus was "the kingdom of heaven is at hand." Jesus Christ's entire ministry was focused on the idea that "the kingdom of heaven is at hand." The disciples became powerfully effective because their focus continued to remain on the fact that "the kingdom of heaven is at hand." All these years later, if we are to be effective, then our focus as well must be on "the kingdom of heaven is at hand." It is not somewhere else. It is not here or there. Instead, it is within us. It is a place where God's will is done on earth just as it is in heaven. If we will only seek first the kingdom, then we (like the early disciples) will become emboldened enigmas, demonstrating puzzling, mysterious, and almost inexplicable behavior as the power of the Holy Spirit flows through us and the miraculous happens all around us. Then we—as adopted orphans—can also go change our world.

"The kingdom of heaven is like treasure hidden in a field."

Matthew 13:44

14   Seeking the Kingdom

Hidden Treasure

There once was a kingdom that both was and was not yet.

"Seek first the kingdom of God and his righteousness, and all these things will be added to you" (Matthew 6:33). Such a simple yet powerful statement given by Jesus Christ to assure his followers that they need not worry about what they would eat, what they would drink, or what they would wear. But make no mistake; all these "other things" were very pressing issues for the Jewish people at the time. In a time of national oppression, poverty, and poor health, the common Jewish people were eager to find a king who would give them relief, heal their diseases, and feed their hunger. The Pharisees, Sadducees, Priests, and other religious leaders were longing for a return to some of the power they had lost under captivity. They were so focused on their own status and the earlier promise of God naming Israel as a kingdom of priests and a holy nation over the rest of the world that they ignored the conditions that God had listed for that blessing, and they also ignored their promise to keep all his commandments. After such a long time in captivity and especially during the time of Roman oppression, the Jewish zealots were excited for the potential to overthrow the Roman government and establish their own earthly kingdom.

Each of these different factions for their own reasons were looking forward to the coming of a messiah, a savior. They remembered the prophesy of Daniel stating that an everlasting kingdom would come to replace the kingdoms of Babylon, Medo-Persia, Greece, and now finally the Roman Empire. The common people longed for a miraculous kingdom that could meet all their physical needs. The religious leaders wanted a political kingdom that would give them position and authority. The zealots wanted a military overthrow that would give them independence and personal liberty to do whatever they wanted. None of these groups were prepared for a hidden kingdom that would give them none of the above. They were certainly not ready to hear from a "king" who would directly challenge their assumptions and openly say that those kinds of kingdoms were not the reason he came.

The people of Israel all "supposed that the kingdom of God was going to appear immediately" (Luke 19:11). Because of this assumption that was obvious in the expectations and statements of the crowds, Jesus began to tell them parables that made it clear that the kingdom was not yet. He told them the parable of a nobleman who before he went away called his servants and gave them differing amounts of money and then told them to put the money to work until he returned (Luke 19:12-27). He had already told them the parable of the landowner who planted a vineyard and then went away. Periodically the landowner sent servants and finally his son to collect the landowner's share of the fruit; however, the tenants beat and even killed the servants and son (Matthew 21:33-41). He also told them the parable of the wheat and tares in which the landowner told his servants to let the tares (weeds) grow with the good wheat, which would be separated from the tares later (Matthew 13:24-30). All these parables made it clear that the king would go away and not come until a much later time. So, Jesus was clearly stating that the kingdom was definitely "not yet."

Even so, being asked by the Pharisees when the kingdom of God was coming, he answered them, "The kingdom of God is not coming with signs to be observed; nor will they say, 'Lo, here it is!' or 'There! For behold, the kingdom of God is in the mist of you'" (Luke 17:20-21). In other words, it was already there because Jesus Christ was there. His presence signaled the arrival of the kingdom. In fact, when the Pharisees accused Jesus of casting out demons by the power of Beelzebub (Matthew 12:24), he responded by stating that "If I drive out demons by Beelzebub, by whom do your people drive them out? So then, they will be your judges. But if it is by the Spirit of God that I drive out demons, then the kingdom of God has come upon you (Matthew 12:27-28). Once again, he stated that the kingdom has already come.

This is an essential part of the wonderful mystery of the kingdom of heaven. For as we have seen the kingdom both has already come and still it is not yet. As humans we so often fall into the trap of believing easy polarized sound bites and believing life's issues can be limited to an either/or situation. Jesus clearly stated— much to the confusion of the religious leaders around him—that this is a both/and situation. The kingdom both is now and is not yet. So, he highlighted prophecies that were already being fulfilled about the kingdom, and yet at the same time he talked about the end times and how some prophecies about the kingdom would not take place until way in the future.

This mysterious back-and-forth way of communicating made some crowds want to throw him off a cliff (Luke 4:29). Other crowds wanted to crown him immediately by force (John 6:15). Then, on yet another occasion, another crowd had picked up stones to stone him (John 8:59). It was not just the crowds who were struggling with these opposing positions on the kingdom of heaven. Jesus' style of communication and seemingly contradictory statements were maddening to the chief priests and other religious leaders as well. It was so maddening that they decided their best way to deal with him was to kill him—this from the supposed keepers of Mosaic Law that clearly stated, "Thou shalt not kill" (Exodus 20:13). Even the Roman prefect (governor), Pontius Pilate, was baffled by Jesus' position on this matter. As a result of his confusion, he washed his hands of the whole affair, wanting nothing to do with it. Through all this, Jesus clearly communicated about a coming future kingdom, which Christians often refer to as the "blessed hope." Then he would do a 180-degree turn and talk about the kingdom being at hand—immediately in the here and now of our everyday lives.

Perhaps one of the greatest shortcomings of many believers in the modern church is the failure to recognize that the kingdom of heaven is not just our future hope but is also currently at hand. Another one of the many mysteries that we often struggle with is how something can currently exist and can also not yet be fully realized—particularly in our day and time when we are so focused on end products and wanting them quickly. However, God has always been an extremely patient God of process. He had very plainly told us that the kingdom of heaven would be like a mustard seed starting exceedingly small and growing to fill the whole earth.

The kingdom of heaven was, is, and will be very powerfully real. Even so, it started with just one man, the incarnate son of the living God, Jesus Christ. Then it grew from 12 disciples, through 120 of the faithful in the upper room, and 500 followers on the Mount of Ascension, to 3,000 converts on the day of Pentecost. It has grown to millions of believers today and continues to grow. And yet "not everyone who says, Lord, Lord, will enter the kingdom of heaven, but only the one who does the will of the Father who is in heaven" (Matthew 7:21). Even though many individuals claim to be a Christian, not all recognize the kingdom being as active in their lives as it was in the lives of the early disciples. Ultimately, we, like they, must seek first the kingdom and not the miracles, signs, wonders, power, or authority. Those other things are the things that belong to God. If we will seek first his kingdom, he will gladly and freely bestow them upon us. Then, like the disciples, we will find that they will just automatically be signs that follow us.

Unfortunately, it is hard to seek first the kingdom of heaven when we—as a modern church—have such a limited under-standing of the kingdom. Often, just like in the days of Jesus Christ, we are looking for a kingdom that meets our expectations rather than looking for *his* kingdom. How do you seek something if you do not really know what it looks like? Furthermore, if you do not really know what it looks like, even if you do find it you might just walk on past because you don't recognize what you are looking at. Even worse—once found—the kingdom might be rejected because we feel that it requires too much of us. If you find yourself in that last camp, Jesus lovingly reminds us that "his yoke is easy, and his burden is light" (Matthew 11:30). Although there is still a yoke and a burden, it is so much better than the cost of the alternatives. That is why Jesus so carefully laid out the parables as a roadmap to kingdom living.

So, if as we have learned, the rock not hewn by human hand is to come down and replace the other kingdoms of this world, and if the kingdom comes originally as a small rock and only later grows to fill the whole earth, and if the rock is Christ Jesus come to establish his kingdom through relationships, then how do we embrace the kingdom? Fundamentally we need to ask, "What is the nature of the kingdom?" and "How do I go about seeking it first?"

So, for a just little while let us explore what God's Word says about this kingdom.

- *To see it, you must be born again.* "I tell you the truth, no one can see the kingdom of God unless he be born again" (John 3:3).

- *You must receive it like a little child.* "I tell you the truth, anyone who will not receive the kingdom of God like a little child will never enter it" (Mark 10:15).
- *It is within you.* Once having been asked by the Pharisees when the kingdom of God would come, Jesus replied, "The kingdom of God does not come with your careful observation, nor will people say, 'Here it is,' or 'There it is,' because the kingdom of God is within you" (Luke 17:20-21).
- *It requires doing God's will.* "Not everyone who says to me, 'Lord, Lord,' will enter the kingdom of heaven, but only he who does the will of my Father who is in heaven" (Matthew 7:21).
- *It requires obedience.* "This then is how you should pray: 'Our Father in heaven, hallowed be your name, your kingdom come, your will be done, on earth as it is in heaven'" (Matthew 6:9-10). If the kingdom of heaven is a place where the will of the Father is done on earth as it is in heaven, then the only way that is possible is through obedience. That is why, God stresses that "obedience is better than sacrifice" (1 Samuel 15:22).
- *It requires discipline and endurance.* "They preached the good news in that city and won a large number of disciples. Then they returned to Lystra, Iconium, and Antioch, strengthening the disciples and encouraging them to remain true to the faith. 'We must go through many hardships to enter the kingdom of God' they said" (Acts 14:21-22).
- *It is not something we just talk about for the future, but it is something we do now through the power of the Holy Spirit.* "For the kingdom of God is not a matter of talk but of power" (1 Corinthians 4:20). "But if I drive out demons by the Spirit of God, then the kingdom of God has come upon you" (Matthew 12:28).
- *It has to do with righteousness and being in relationship in such a way as to be pleasing to God and approved by men.* "For the kingdom of God is not a matter of eating and drinking, but of righteousness, peace and joy in the Holy Spirit, because anyone who serves Christ in this way is pleasing to God and approved by men" (Romans 14:17-18).
- *It is about relationships.* "One of the teachers of the law came and heard them debating. Noticing Jesus had given them a good

answer, he asked him, 'Of all the commandments, which is the most important?' 'The most important one,' answered Jesus, 'is this: Hear of Israel, the Lord our God, the Lord is one. Love the Lord your God with all your heart and with all your soul and with all your mind and with all your strength. The second is this, Love your neighbor as yourself. There is no commandment greater than these.' 'Well said, teacher,' the man replied. 'You are right in saying that God is one and there is no other but him. To love him with all your heart, with all your understanding and with all your strength, and to love your neighbor as yourself is more important than all burnt offerings and sacrifices.' When Jesus saw that he had answered wisely, he said to him, 'You are not far from the kingdom" (Mark 12:28-34).

Therefore, entering the kingdom of God is about a life change that begins when we are born again. It is something within us that allows us to live lives that are pleasing to God and that are approved by men. This is accomplished by carefully doing the will of God through a life of obedience, discipline, and endurance. Most of all, it is something that places an emphasis on the importance of relationships and the love that sustains those relationships.

Yes, we are supposed to look forward to the "blessed hope" which is the prophesied second coming of the Lord and Savior Jesus Christ. Paul has described this future event by stating that, "The Lord himself will come down from heaven, with a loud command, with the voice of the archangel and with the trumpet call of God, and the dead in Christ will rise first. After that, we who are still alive and left will be caught up together with them in the clouds to meet the Lord in the air. And so we will be with the Lord forever" (1 Thessalonians 4:16-17). Jesus told the disciples and us "that I am going there to prepare a place for you. And if I go and prepare a place for you, I will come back and take you to be with me that you also may be where I am" (John 14:2-3). So the "blessed hope we have is that we are destined to live with Jesus in the future kingdom of heaven. But we dare not wait for the future kingdom by neglecting the kingdom that is at hand. The kingdom starts in the here and now the moment every new believer accepts Jesus Christ as their Lord and Savior.

Part of the mystery of the kingdom of heaven is that it is not just something that we wait for in the future but something we are actively involved with in the here and now of our everyday lives. It is a transformation that allows us to be in a powerfully dynamic relationship with God and with others. Even though "it does not yet appear what we shall be" (1 John 3:2), we are actively in the process of becoming. The kingdom is within you and is both now and is not yet. God's purpose is to establish a living unshakable kingdom that will never end, where his will is done here on earth as it is in heaven. That kingdom is at hand within us. Then, as we live out kingdom principles, others are compelled to join us on the shared journey, helping the kingdom grow. Being actively involved in the kingdom now is yet another part of the mystery of the kingdom of heaven that we are to be stewards of.

"In reading this, then, you will be able to understand my insight into the mystery of Christ, which was not made known to men in other generations as it has now been revealed by the Spirit to God's holy apostles and prophets. This mystery is that through the gospel the Gentiles are heirs together with Israel, members together of one body, and sharers together in the promise in Christ Jesus."

Ephesians 3:2-6

15	Relationships

The Covert Kingdom

There once was a realm that was difficult to perceive.

When something is covert, it is secretive, hidden, and hard to see. When it is overt, it is obvious. The people who lived during the time Jesus Christ was on earth desperately longed for an overt kingdom to meet their pressing needs. They wanted an immediate and obvious kingdom to replace the Roman government that was in power at the time.

But that is not what Jesus Christ came to bring. His kingdom was not a political kingdom nor a territorial or regional kingdom. It was not a military kingdom, a utopian kingdom, or a philosophical kingdom. It was not a democracy, a monarchy, an aristocracy, or an oligarchy. It was not communism or socialism. It also was not authoritarianism or totalitarianism.

In fact, it was to be a kingdom like no other ever in human history. It would be a relational kingdom. As such the nature of the relationships would be like no other in history as well. For the head of the kingdom would be a benevolent despot who through servant leadership did only that which was in the best interest of his subjects. On the other hand, his subjects would all be volunteers who would freely choose to live under the absolute rule of this unique kind of leader. Even more amazing would be the nature of the subject's relationships with each other. Although the relationships would be awkward and difficult at first, over time and with the developing maturity of the subjects, they would also take on the servant leadership qualities modeled by the benevolent despot.

To even attempt such a kingdom from all earthly standards seemed like sheer madness. Relationships are risky and they are messy. Human beings are notoriously good at letting others down and that is even when they are at their best. At their worst they are harmful, abusive, jealous, unforgiving, resentful, cruel, and murderous. It is not in our fallen nature to do what is best for others and take on servant qualities. Even so, that is how the mystery of the kingdom of God was designed to proceed. That is why for the kingdom to work Jesus had clearly stated that it would need to be defined by love and unity. In fact, his last prayer in the garden of Gethsemane was "that all of them may be one, Father, just as you are in me, and I am in you. May they also be in us so that the world may believe that you have sent me" (John 17:21). In other words, the only way people would be able to see that this was indeed a kingdom is if somehow its subjects could get past the risky and messy nature of most relationships and move on to something far more powerful.

Risky or not, Jesus kept revealing these ideas as part of the mystery of God's kingdom. Messy or not, he also very directly challenged his followers to make the attempt to enter this kind of a kingdom. But this covert kingdom and its principles were not what the religious leaders wanted to hear. As such, they often went about trying to find ways to trap Jesus with his own words so they could discount or ignore him. On one such occasion, they asked him which was the greatest command. This was intended to be a setup because they thought that no matter what he said, they could admonish him for not addressing other commands. Their goal was to tarnish his reputation and "knock him down a few pegs" in front of the crowds.

Jesus—in perceiving their intent—answered them by replying, "Love the Lord your God with all your heart and with all your soul and with all your mind. This is the first and greatest command. And the second is like it: Love your neighbor as yourself. All of the law and the prophets hang on these two commandments" (Matthew 22:37-40). That last little phrase effectively shut down the religious leaders in their attempt to discredit him, for if you genuinely love God and your neighbors in this way, you will keep all the other commandments. But even beyond settling the issue with the religious leaders of the day, Jesus was in effect saying that the mystery of this kingdom is all about relationships. All the laws from the Old Testament and all the issues of grace from the New Testament were about making relationships work the way they were originally intended by God to work.

We see this reflected yet again in the writings of Paul when he states that "The entire law is summed up in a single command: Love your neighbor as yourself" (Galatians 5:14). This is the key to the mystery of the kingdom of Heaven. It is a kingdom of relationships: first our relationship with God and then our relationships with others.

Just as "The Church" is not a physical building, but instead is made up of the people who are united in fellowship as the "body of Christ," so the kingdom is not going to be a physical kingdom but a relational kingdom.

This new and unique kind of kingdom would reside within and between people. It would be a covert kingdom. That is because unless you were paying attention to what was happening between individuals, you would not see the kingdom. So how can one become aware of such a kingdom? Jesus had answered that question when he said, "By this, everyone will know that you are my disciples, if you love one another" (John 13:35). The demonstration of love in relationships is how the kingdom will be made visible in the here and now of our everyday lives. That becomes a bit of a challenge because the world throws around so many different definitions of love.

So, if we want to see the kingdom, what do we look for? Fortunately for us the Word says that "prophecy never had its origin in the human will, but prophets, though human, spoke from God as they were carried along by the Holy Spirit" (2 Peter 1:21). It also says that "all Scripture is God-breathed and is useful for teaching, rebuking, correcting, and training in righteousness so that the servant of God may be thoroughly equipped for every good work" (2 Timothy 3:16-17). As such we should look to the Scriptures to see how God defines the love that we shall be known by.

In a very famous passage in the Bible called "the love chapter," we are given a definition of love that stands out as timeless and unique. It says, "Love is patient, love is kind. It does not envy, it does not boast, it is not proud. It does not dishonor others, it is not self-seeking, it is not easily angered, it keeps no record of wrongs. Love does not delight in evil but rejoices with the truth. It always protects, always hopes, always perseveres. Love never fails" (1 Corinthians 13:4-8). So here in these few words, we have a road map for how to treat God and others if we want to see the relational kingdom.

All this is well and good. However, seeing the kingdom manifested in our day and time has become much more difficult. In this post-modern world in which we now live, the greatest challenge is that love has been redefined by our current culture. Far too often the voices all around have redefined love as acceptance, tolerance, and inclusion. I want to be very clear that I am not trying to make any political statement here. What I do want to address is that there is a big difference between patience, kindness, and not dishonoring others versus acceptance, tolerance, and inclusion. Every parent who has ever really loved their child knows that these last three items are not always real love.

Real love absolutely cannot accept all behavior. This is because some behaviors are harmful, spiteful, selfish to the detriment of others, full of undue risk, ignoring of consequences, and destructive. Real love understands that building character over the long haul is more important than immediate acceptance.

Real love is not tolerant of all beliefs. If I believe that I can fly without a plane, I am highly likely to act on that belief and suffer the very real consequences of gravity. Real love challenges erroneous beliefs to protect those who are loved.

Real love does not include all people. While this may sound very provocative or controversial in our current culture, it is none the less true. If a parent really loves their child, they will not require them to include the bully, the exploiter, the pedophile, etc. In the fallen world we live in, not everyone is safe to be around.

While real love is patient, kind, and does not dishonor others, it also does indeed set limits, provide boundaries, and says "NO" to a wide range of issues. Even when it may not be appreciated, real love intervenes when it is necessary to do so to keep someone safe or to help them grow. That is why in the book of Proverbs it states that "the one who loves their children is careful to discipline them" (Proverbs 13:24).

I do want to be clear here that young, immature Christians in very risky and messy relationships may use the statements I have made above—such as not accepting all behaviors, not tolerating all beliefs, and not including all people—as an excuse for racism, bigotry, and divisiveness. In our ever shrinking and globalized post-modern world, we have seen far too many examples of just that.

Part of what makes this kingdom realm so difficult to perceive is that too many are using their own definitions of love and trying to set their own limits and boundaries. Because as human beings we have such a poor record of how we set limits, create boundaries, and say "no," we should be very careful to make sure we are following God's guidance on safe limits and not just skewing our choices and behavior with our own personal filters and biases.

The Bible clearly says that we are to study to show ourselves approved as someone "who correctly handles the word of truth" (2 Timothy 2:15). If in our relational kingdom we do that and demonstrate the qualities that are listed in the love chapter, then others will sit up and take notice. What they will then see is not division, divisiveness, racism, and bigotry, but instead it will be the kind of love that Jesus said we would be known by. It will be the kind of love that brings the unity that he prayed so earnestly for.

In this covert kingdom composed of so many risky and messy relationships, there is only one thing that will move us more fully into that kingdom reality of love and unity. As Jesus so often stated, there is only one thing that will bring the kingdom of heaven at hand, and that one thing is Christian maturity—or as Paul states it, growing from glory to glory into the image of Christ. We are clearly all works in progress, which is why we are supposed to be quick to forgive. This is also why Jesus told the parable of the wheat and the tares. In telling the servants not to pull out the weeds just yet, Jesus was acknowledging that in all the messiness that comes along with the developmental process of maturity, it would be too easy to pull up some of the wheat thinking it was just a weed. That is why he is long suffering and patient; he is not willing that any should perish.

If Jesus—our example—is careful not to be premature about his process of separating us out, then we too as his disciples should be careful not to rush to judgement of others. Instead, we are to spur one another onto love and good works. We are to be unified in our efforts for building strong relationships and, thus, the kingdom. If we are ever going to move beyond the risky and messy nature of relationships to something much more powerful that is infused with love and unity, we must fully embrace the process of maturing in Christ. If we are really longing to see this covert kingdom, then we as believers must fully embrace a developmental model of personal spiritual growth.

Jesus challenged us to do so when he gave us the great commission. He stated that we should "therefore go and make disciples of all nations, baptizing them in the name of the Father and of the Son and of the Holy Spirit, and teaching them to obey everything I have commanded you" (Matthew 28:19-20). Unfortunately, we have far too often watered down the Great Commission to simply going and making converts of all nations. While the contemporary church has done a great job of winning converts the world over, we are not as effective at discipleship. A disciple follows in their master's footstep, learns through example, grows to become more effective in their ability to emulate the master's teachings and lifestyle, and ultimately is able to carry on with making new disciples themselves. All of this requires time, effort, dedication, and above all else the one thing that Jesus himself had emphasized, which is obedience.

Obedience is the real key to this covert kingdom of relationships. If we are ever as a group of people going to be able to enter the kingdom at hand, if we are ever going to be able to live out the love and the unity that is the hallmark of this kingdom, if we are ever going to be able to flesh out the parables in our everyday lifestyle; then it will only happen as we are all drawn together in Jesus Christ and obeying his commands and decrees. After all, this covert, relational kingdom does have a king. The kingdom is not just a form of fire insurance or a get-out-of-hell-free card; it is a real kingdom with a very real and powerful sovereign who is very much in charge. He has our best interest at heart. By faith, we must choose to believe that. Then, with every fiber of our being, we must act on that belief by freely choosing to live under the absolute rule of this incredibly unique kind of leader.

Paradox

God's Process

"It is the glory of God to conceal a matter, to search out a matter is the glory of kings."

Proverbs 25:2

16   **The Harsh Punishments of God**

Who Done It?

As we approach the mysteries of God's kingdom, we find—just like with all great mysteries—the big question always is, "who done it?" Whether it is a murder mystery or some other form of mystery, there is always a central figure that is the pivotal character.

As we have seen so far, God the Father had both concealed and then carefully revealed his plan for the ages (the Mystery of Godliness) in the many puzzles that he presented to mankind throughout history. Then his Son, Jesus Christ, both concealed and strategically revealed the nature and purpose of his ministry (the Mystery of the Kingdom of Heaven) in the many parables that he shared with the crowds and with his disciples. It was for our benefit and God's glory that these things were concealed. Just as God would be found only when we search for him with all our heart, so too the kingdom would be found only when we seek it first.

In revealing our new nature and destiny in this kingdom, God's word in the King James Version states he has "made us kings and priests unto God and his Father" (Revelation 1:5-6). Therefore, now since he has made us kings and priests, it is to our benefit and glory to search out these matters. It is not something we should do when we get around to it or when it is convenient. Instead, if we really want to be part of this kingdom of relationships, it is something we should seek first and with all our hearts. God asks us to go on a journey of discovery and earnestly search out these things. Inevitably when we do, we run into some of the more challenging mysteries that it was God's glory to conceal—mysteries that were hidden from the foundations of the world and that were hiding everywhere in plain sight. When we approach these mysteries, we find issues that may at first be difficult to understand about God and his kingdom. Even so, remember that God has "given the full assurance of the understanding of the mysteries of God" (Colossians 2:2).

If we embrace this journey of discovery, we will find that many of the more challenging issues of the kingdom are presented to us in the form of a paradox, "a seemingly absurd or self-contradictory

147

statement or proposition that when investigated or explained may prove to be to be well founded or true" (Oxford Dictionary). When we come across difficult paradoxes found in God's word and we commit to explore them, we—through his grace—discover hidden truth.

So, how does one reconcile the paradox of an unchanging and loving God, full of mercy and grace, who then sometimes seems to do a 180-degree turn and act differently? Why would a God who is patient and longsuffering on more than one occasion seem to step out of character and exact what seems to us to be a swift and harsh punishment? This challenging paradox has been yet another stumbling block for a considerable number of individuals who have heard about some of the stories in the Bible.

There are many times that are recorded when God did so, particularly in the Old Testament. In fact, because this is so, people sometimes claim there is a difference between the God of the Old Testament and the God of the New Testament. That claim is mistaken because God in his word clearly says, "I the Lord do not change" (Malachi 3:6). It is the same God that we find throughout the Bible. Even so, because of the harsh punishments recorded in God's Word, this presents a difficulty for some individuals. For example, in the Old Testament we read the story of Lot's wife, who "looked back, and she became a pillar of salt" (Genesis 19:26). We can also read the story of a portion of the nation of Israel who sinned against God and "the ground under the men opened. It was as if the earth opened its mouth and swallowed them" (Numbers 16:32). These are just a few examples. But even in the New Testament we read the story of Ananias and Sapphira who dropped dead at Peter's feet because they lied to the Holy Spirit about how much they were giving to the young Christian church (Acts 5:1-11). Seemingly harsh punishments are not relegated to the Old Testament only. So, on our journey of discovery as we pursue God, pursue his kingdom, and try to understand these revelations of God, how do we make sense of all this?

Sometimes it may seem as though God administers very harsh punishments, but God has an extremely good reason for everything he does. This truth is so obvious that it is not often stated. However, scripture records incidents where God's reasons were not always clear or easy to comprehend. There are isolated incidents where God, who is long suffering, seemed to step totally out of character. He personally judged and, at least from our perspective, swiftly executed harsh punishment on both individuals and groups. What are God's reasons for such harsh punishments?

The Example of Lot's Wife

We have already established that God was active in history producing dramas through foreshadowing in the lives of men and women, through the epic drama of the entire nation of Israel, and even through the order or succession of many kingdoms. Therefore, let us for a moment examine another drama recorded in the story of Lot living in Sodom and Gomorrah. There can be no doubt that this was a drama produced by God because of confirmation by Jesus Christ himself. When the evil nature of the men in Sodom and Gomorrah became the same as the nature of wicked men in the end times and when a righteous man could live in this environment and still be called righteous and just, God produced his drama.

We know this is what happened because Peter states, "If he condemned the cities of Sodom and Gomorrah by burning them to ashes, and made them an example of what is going to happen to the ungodly; and if he rescued Lot, a righteous man, who was distressed by the filthy lives of lawless men (for that righteous man, living among them day after day, was tormented in his righteous soul by the lawless deeds he saw and heard)—if this is so, then the Lord knows how to rescue the godly from trials and to hold the unrighteous for punishment on the day of judgement" (2 Peter 2:6-8). God provided this script to Lot and his family via angelic messengers. If you recall, he intentionally sent two angels with extremely specific instructions. Lot and his wife were told to "flee for your life! Do not look behind you, nor stop anywhere in the plain; flee to the hills, lest you be swept away (Genesis 19:17). The Bible records that Lot's wife did look back and was turned into a pillar of salt.

Why turn Lot's wife into a pillar of salt? Did God deal too harshly with Lot's wife? After all, perhaps she was only exhibiting a mother's compassion for her future sons-in-law back in the city. They had not left the city because they thought Lot was joking when he warned them. Human logic, by itself, will not allow us to understand God's reasons for turning Lot's wife into a pillar of salt, but the spiritual events portrayed in the drama will.

Jesus himself made a statement that explains the drama. When referring to his second coming and God's judgment on the earth, he said "he that is on the housetop . . . let him not come down . . .he that is in the field . . . not return back—Remember Lot's wife (Luke 17:28-32).

We love to hear that God is patient, kind, longsuffering, full of grace, quick to forgive, and compassionate. But in Psalms 7:11, the Bible declares that God is also a just judge and that he is angry with the wicked every day. Even though we do not always want to hear that about God, it is nevertheless true. So, when God could no longer tolerate the sin in Sodom and Gomorrah, he pronounced his judgment on them. Unfortunately, Lot's wife had lived there long enough that her attentions were turned in their direction as well, so she also received their judgment. Paul, in explaining how this relates to us, states that "these things happened to them as examples and were written down as warnings for us, on whom the culmination of the ages has come. So, if you think you are standing firm, be careful that you don't fall" (1 Corinthians 10:11-12).

In God's drama, Lot's wife was in a type or foreshadowing of the rapture. Her feet had left the ground. Halfway to heaven her thoughts suddenly returned to the earth as she became concerned about the things behind her. Her part in this drama shows us clearly that we should be focused on the things of God and not be turning our attentions elsewhere. As a result, God judged Lot's wife because Christians in the rapture must have faith and expectation for the things ahead of them and not the things of this earth. And that is why Jesus says, "remember Lot's wife." Lot's wife was turned into a pillar of salt to prevent those watching the drama from concluding that her action was what God had planned. The judgment was harsh because the correct action was important for our understanding. God does not produce dramas for unimportant events. Each is a matter of grave, spiritual concern.

It would be presumptuous to pretend to know for certain the ways of God, for he has stated through the prophet Isaiah that "As the heavens are higher than the earth, so are my ways higher than your ways and my thoughts than your thoughts (Isaiah 55:8-9). But when the Creator of mysteries reveals his thoughts and his ways through the living word of his only Son Jesus Christ, then we—even if only for a moment—have been given a glimpse into these matters. In this instance, Jesus reveals that the harsh punishment on Lot's wife was because God was using her family's lives as an example for the rest of mankind. Unfortunately, she deviated from the script that he had carefully provided. It is easier to understand the paradox of a loving and longsuffering God who would turn around and execute swift judgement if you consider that he loves all those who would come afterward too much not to warn them of the consequences of their behavior. The paradox always has purpose. So, when we see other examples of swift or harsh judgment in the Bible, we should not back away from God or decide we do not like this kind of a God. Instead, we should sit up, take notice, and ask what message God is specifically trying to communicate.

Therefore, as we more deeply pursue the mystery of Godliness and the mystery of the kingdom of heaven, let us explore yet another of the seemingly harsh punishments recorded in the Bible. In fact, to address this part of the mystery of which we are to be stewards, let's briefly examine a puzzle, several parables, and a paradox.

The Puzzle

Early in the ministry of Elisha, there is recorded another one of the harsh punishments of God. In that story we read "From there Elisha went up to Bethel. As he was walking along the road, some youths came out of the town and jeered at him. 'Go on up, you baldhead!' they said. 'Go on up, you baldhead!' He turned around, looked at them, and called down a curse on them in the name of the LORD. Then two bears came out of the woods and mauled forty-two of the youths. And he went on to Mount Carmel and from there returned to Samaria" (2 Kings 2:23-25).

Was Elisha just overly sensitive about his own baldness? Why—at such an early point in his ministry having only recently received the mantle of anointing from Elijah—would he even bother to acknowledge the young men, let alone call a curse down on them? Notice that the prophet simply called down a curse on them as part of his ministry and relationship to God and then immediately went on about his business in the next couple of locations. He did not pray for a specific response from God, yet God's response was to have two bears come out of the woods. Why in response to Elisha's prayer would a loving God sentence 42 adolescents to be mauled by bears for doing what adolescents tend to do (e.g., taunting and teasing). In and of itself this seems to be a particularly harsh response. To

151

understand this puzzle in the form of a harsh punishment, we need to dive a little deeper into the background of this story.

You may remember that Elijah, Elisha's predecessor had defeated king Ahab's prophets of Baal on mount Carmel by calling down fire from heaven to consume his sacrifice. Afterwards many of the prophets of Baal were either killed or run off. However, once Ahab had died, his son Ahaziah returned to his father's practices. "He did evil in the eyes of the Lord because he followed the ways of his father and mother and of Jeroboam, son of Nebat, who caused Israel to sin" (1 Kings 22:52). Ahaziah served Baal and provoked God to anger just as his father had done. He reinstituted the Ashura poles, temple prostitution, detestable sexual practices, and Baal worship throughout Israel. This was particularly true in Bethel, which was originally named by Jacob as the house of God. However, first under Ahab's reign and then under Ahaziah's reign, Bethel had become a stronghold for all these evil behaviors that God hated.

One day King Ahaziah fell through a hole in the roof and seriously injured himself. Unfortunately, as was his practice, instead of asking God for help, he sent a messenger to consult Baal-Zebub. At God's prompting, Elijah intercepted the messenger and told him to tell the king that because he did not consult God, he would not leave the bed he was lying on before he died.

In response to this unfavorable prophesy, three times the king sent a different captain with 50 men to confront Elijah, saying "Man of God, come down." They had intended to kill him once he came down off the mountain. Each time Elijah—under the anointing of God—had said, "If I am a man of God, then may fire fall from heaven and consume you" (2 Kings 1:10-12). The first two times this literally happened, the men were burned up. When the third captain came—having seen what had happened to the first and second groups—he asked for mercy. At that, the angel of God freed Elijah to have mercy on the men and to go speak to the king in person. When the evil king finally heard Elijah's message, he died.

It was with this as a backdrop that the prophets of Baal and their adolescent youth, who now on multiple occasions had been defeated, out of anger continued to harass Elijah and Elisha. On several occasions the company of the prophets of Baal at Bethel and at Jericho came to Elisha and prophesied saying, "do you know that God is going to take your master today?" In response Elisha said, "Yes, I know, but do not speak of it" (2 Kings 2:3). Earlier Elijah had asked what Elisha wanted from him. In response Elisha had asked for a double portion of the spirit of God on his life. Elisha had been promised that if he were with Elijah when he went up into heaven, then he would have what he desired. Therefore, Elisha already knew that Elijah would be taken by God. Even so, it was not the place or the time for the false prophets of Baal to be addressing this.

When we finally get to the point in history when Elijah was going to be caught up into heaven in a chariot of fire and the mantle of anointing was to be passed on to Elisha, there were 50 men and their company, which most likely included these adolescents, standing by the Jordan watching the entire event. I always assumed as a little child that this ascension in a chariot of fire and a whirlwind happened in the middle of an isolated desert somewhere. But it did not happen that way. The entire audience mentioned above watched the parting of the Jordan river, Elijah and Elisha walking across on dry land, the chariot and the whirlwind coming down out of heaven and returning to heaven with Elijah, Elisha receiving Elijah's mantle, and then parting the waters of the Jordan and walking back across the river on dry ground once again. What they saw with their own eyes was unmistakable. The same spirit of power that had been on Elijah— which enabled him to outperform, more accurately prophesy, do supernatural miracles, and just simply make their lives miserable— was now on his successor Elisha. That was the last thing the prophets of Baal wanted.

At this point in the story, Elisha traveled to a nearby town and cleansed the water so that the town's people would no longer be sick and their land would be productive. Afterward he traveled back to Bethel and that was when the obnoxious adolescents who were the sons of the prophets began again with their taunts and harassment. In effect they were prophesying that Elisha should "go up" just as Elijah had done before. This would have suited them fine to be rid of the true prophet of God that had made their own ineffective efforts at religiosity and their detestable practices look so weak and powerless. Apparently both Elisha and God were done with the prophets of Baal and their meddling. And so, Elisha pronounces a curse on them.

The issue of a Godly curse is not an isolated thing here in the Old Testament. In the New Testament it states that "All who rely on observing the law are under a curse" (Galatians 3:10). It also says that

"If anyone does not love the Lord—a curse be on him" (1 Corinthians 15:22). Finally in Matthew it says, "If anyone will not welcome you or listen to your words, shake the dust off your feet when you leave that home or town. I tell you the truth, it will be more bearable for Sodom and Gomorrah on the day of judgment than for that town" (Matthew 10:14-16). So, we see that those who set themselves in opposition to God inevitably find themselves under a curse. The puzzle is how and why God chooses to fulfill this specific curse by having bears maul the jeering adolescents. It is clearly one of the seemingly harsh punishments designed to get our attention. But what is the message that is being conveyed?

The Parables

As we look at this issue of what God is trying to convey, it will help to also look at several other stories in the Bible that may also be hard to understand at first. In relating the classic parable of the talents or the bags of gold, Jesus states a proposition that might be considered by some to be very disturbing with our current society's emphasis on equity and social justice. The parable involves someone who was to be appointed king. However, some of his subjects did not want him to be king. Even so, he was made the king. As such, he sent for men that were given five bags of gold, two bags of gold, and one bag of gold respectively. The man with five bags invested it wisely and gained five more bags of gold. The man with two bags also invested wisely and gained two more bags of gold. Finally, the man with one bag went and hid it for safe keeping and did nothing else with it.

When the owner came back and asked to see what had been done with his money, he was pleased with the first two gentlemen but angry with the last. As a result, he took the one bag of gold from the last man and gave it to the first man who already had ten. At the end of the parable he says, "For whoever has will be given more, and they will have an abundance. Whoever does not have, even that they have will be taken from them" (Matthew 25:29). In a similar parable recorded by Luke, the people reacted by saying, "'Sir, he already has ten!'" "He replied, 'I tell you that to everyone who has, more will be given, but as for the one who has nothing, even what he has will be taken away. But those enemies of mine who did not want me to be king over them—bring them here and kill them in front of me'" (Luke 19:25-27).

From our earthly way of thinking, this seems to be a paradox that does not line up with what we call social justice and that also seems to be harsh. However, if we look at the context of the parable, we can begin to understand it. God was rewarding those who were diligent and faithful with what they had been given. But on the other hand, he removed even what little they did have from those who did not produce an increase.

Listen to another parable. There was a landowner who planted a vineyard. He put a wall around it, dug a winepress in it, and built a watchtower. Then he rented the vineyard to some farmers and went away on a journey. When the harvest time approached, he sent his servants to the tenants to collect his fruit. The tenants seized his servants; they beat one, killed another, and stoned a third. Then he sent other servants to them, more than the first time, and the tenants treated them the same way. Last of all, he sent his son to them. "They will respect my son," he said.

But when the tenants saw the son, they said to each other, "This is the heir. Come, let's kill him and take his inheritance." So, they took him and threw him out of the vineyard and killed him. "Therefore, when the owner of the vineyard comes, what will he do to those tenants?" "He will bring those wretches to a wretched end," they replied, "and he will rent the vineyard to other tenants, who will give him his share of the crop at harvest time."

Jesus said to them, "Have you never read in the Scriptures 'The stone the builders rejected has become the cornerstone; the Lord has done this, and it is marvelous in our eyes?' "Therefore, I tell you that the kingdom of God will be taken away from you and given to a people who will produce its fruit. He who falls on this stone will be broken to pieces, but he on whom it falls will be crushed (Matthew 21:33-43).

Once again, we see that those who are entrusted with something in this kingdom must use it to produce an increase.

The Paradox

And finally, the paradox. Jesus wants us to be with him forever in heaven, so he prays to his heavenly Father that God does not take us out of this world but that he protects us from the evil one. Then he goes to heaven and leaves us here on earth. If he wants to be with us, why would he leave us? In trying to explain it to us he says, "Unless I go, the comforter cannot come," but we still struggle with the paradox. What we ultimately learn is that he departs from this earth by leaving his limited earthly form so that he can be with us and dwell within us in his unlimited spirit form. Even so, the paradox is that God wants us to live with him forever, so he goes away and leaves us here on earth.

What Does It All Mean?

What do we learn about God's process for establishing His kingdom from all these issues?

- **From the paradox** we learn that God's method of establishing his kingdom is to leave us here on earth.
- **From the parables** we learn that God the father is leaving the kingdom in the hands of others (basically those he has left here on earth). He specifically tells these parables because the people of his day were thinking that the kingdom of God was going to come as other previous earthly kingdoms had come—with a mighty conquering king who would overthrow the current establishment. They thought that the new king would come and immediately make everything better by doing everything for them and solving all their problems. But as we have learned already, it was going to be a unique relational kingdom that required cooperation and collaboration. We would also have to do our part.
- We learn that the kingdom will be for those who produce fruit. So, while we are here on earth, we must be productive.
- We also learn the kingdom is a process that grows and that if individuals in the kingdom do not produce growth (or worse yet, if they are enemies of the kingdom), then their punishment will be severe.
- **From the puzzle** we learn all of this and something even more important.

If you recall our discussion of the harsh punishments of God, it will help bring new light to this puzzle. Whenever it seems as if a

156

harsh punishment has occurred, we should sit up, take notice, and ask what message God is specifically trying to communicate. More often than not, it is a message of foreshadowing to help us understand future events. In the case of the 42 adolescents and the two bears, the harsh punishment alerts us to a direct analogy and foreshadowing of the story of Jesus Christ and his disciples.

In this story Elijah is an archetype of Jesus Christ, and Elisha is an archetype of his disciples or followers who come after him. The parallels are many, and they are significant.

- **Both stories include a place where the forces of evil—the false prophets—try to prophesy and are told to be quiet.** Elisha had to tell the prophets of Baal to be quiet when they kept asking if Elisha knew that this day Elijah would be "taken up." Later Jesus had to tell the demons called "legion" to be quiet when they tried to prophesy about him being the Son of God. Even though what they were saying was true, it was not their place nor was it the time to be addressing those issues.
- **Both stories emphasize that the follower would do greater things than the forerunner**. Elisha wanted a double portion of the spirit of God that was on Elijah. When you read through the rest of their stories, you see that Elisha did exactly twice the number of supernatural miracles that were evidenced in Elijah's life. Later Jesus says of his disciples, "Very truly I tell you whoever believes in me will do the works I have been doing, and they will do even greater things than these, because I am going to the Father" (John 14:12).
- **Both stories involve a supernatural ascension into heaven**. Elijah is caught up into heaven with a chariot of fire and a whirlwind. Later Jesus is caught up into heaven in front of 500 followers on the mount of ascension.
- **Both stories require a time of tarrying for the enduement of power.** Elijah had told Elisha that if he tarried with him until Elisha left, then he would have what he desired: the mantle of God's anointing. Later Jesus told his disciples to tarry in Jerusalem until they were endued with power (the mantle of the Holy Spirit).

- **Both stories focus on the follower staying behind and carrying on the work of the forerunner**. Elijah told Elisha to stay behind several times (2 Kings 2:2, 4). Also, Jesus prayed that we would stay behind and not be taken out of the world: "My prayer is not that you take them out of the world but that you protect them from the evil one. They are not of the world, even as I am not of it. Sanctify them by the truth; your word is truth. As you sent me into the world, I have sent them into the world" (John 17:15-18).

Now finally we come to an understanding of the harsh punishment of the adolescents. The 42 sons of the prophets of Baal were trying to mess up God's picture by falsely prophesying over Elisha to "go up" or to go away just as Satan would love for us to all go away and not remain here to influence others into the kingdom. They received the harsh punishment of being mauled by bears because it was God's plan for Elisha to stay and do even greater works than his predecessor Elijah. Multiple times in the word of God there are warnings against false prophets. Unfortunately, the 42 youths placed themselves in that very dangerous role. They were directly prophesying against God's will. God—through foreshadowing—was very pointedly illustrating that disciples of Jesus would stay on earth and do even greater things than he had done. God's intent was to leave them as well as us behind here on earth to build the kingdom of God. In fact, Jesus prays not just for those immediate disciples alone but "also for those who believe in [him] through their message" (John 17:20). In other words, his prayer is for you.

Amazingly, we realize that after the incredible complexity and the all-encompassing nature of the heavenly Father's planning—as well as all the amazing work that Jesus Christ has done in atoning for our sins and the incredible teachings that he passed on—he returned to his heavenly Father and left it all in our hands. In obedience to the grand design of God the Father, Jesus the Son invites us to be the central character of his mystery. Undoubtably God the Father's plan is for Jesus Christ to be the central or pivotal person for all time. Even so, as his Son returns to heaven, he shifts the focus from Jesus Christ walking and breathing on planet earth to Jesus Christ in you, the hope of glory.

Therefore, the final answer to "who done it?" is *you*. You, along with the Spirit of God in you, are the process by which the kingdom is being established. Another part of the many mysteries that God has concealed is the fact that he would go to such great lengths to make everything in heaven and earth conform to his plan, send his only begotten Son to begin the process of establishing his kingdom, and then entrust the final outcome to us. It is the ultimate paradox: entrusting the fate and future of the kingdom to frail, flawed human beings who are notorious for messing things up and getting it wrong. And yet that is just what God has done. He not only invites us to step up to the task, but he also empowers us through the Holy Spirit to be able to become more than our flaws and our frailty. No wonder as Christ followers we can rejoice when we are persecuted and when we face tribulations (1 Peter 4:12-13). In fact, in the beatitudes, Jesus has said that you are blessed when that persecution happens, for yours is the kingdom of heaven (Matthew 5:10-12). Just as Christ for the joy set before him endured the cross (Hebrews 12:2), you for the joy set before you can navigate this life and this world. What is the joy set before us? Being part of a volunteer kingdom where our own input helps to establish the final outcome of victory.

"To them God has chosen to make known among the Gentiles the glorious riches of this mystery, which is Christ in you, the hope of glory."

Colossians 1:27

17   **That Which Is Within**

Riddle Me This

The kingdom of God was within Jesus Christ. He gave us a glimpse of that kingdom and what it was like as he walked on this earth and when he taught us to pray: "Our Father who art in heaven, hollowed be thy name. Thy kingdom come, thy will be done, on earth as it is in heaven . . . ." The kingdom was at hand here on earth because Jesus was doing the will of his Father.

As stated earlier, Satan/Lucifer's nature and desires were based on pride, power, mastery, rulership, and being like God. Therefore, God's plan implemented through the life of Jesus Christ would be based upon humility, servanthood, becoming lower than the angels, and taking the form of a man. So at every turn, Jesus would do what Lucifer did not expect: he would become the master of the paradox. For God's will to be done on earth, Jesus had to flip on end all the natural tendencies of the fallen human race and live his life as a divine paradox. Therefore, by the power of the Holy Spirit that was within him, Jesus divested himself of everything that was rightfully his. As a result, he completely lived out these paradoxes:

- The King of Kings became a vulnerable baby of a common Jewish family.
- He who holds the earth, space, and time in his hand—as a fragile young baby himself—had to be held in Mary's arms.
- He is powerful and majestic, yet he still humbled himself.
- He is the master of everything, yet he became a servant.
- He is a limitless God, but he was confined to a limited human body.
- He is the ruler of all creation but became a being lower than the angels.
- He is omnipresent, yet he was limited to one place and time.
- He is the great provider; even so, he had no place to lay his head.
- He is an all-knowing God but was not even known by his own people.

- He is the Prince of Peace, yet turmoil followed his earthly ministry everywhere he went.
- He is the light of the world, and yet the people he loved could not see.
- He became our Kinsman-Redeemer, yet his own people received him not.
- He is our refuge and place of safety; even so, he was rejected, and his life was cut off.
- He is the divine appointer of the priesthood, yet he was persecuted, interrogated, and crucified by the very priests whom he had appointed.
- He is the righteous, true, and just judge, but he was judged by the wicked and corrupt Pontius Pilot.
- He is love, but he was hated and despised by mankind.
- He is a Holy God, yet he was defiled.
- He is full of compassion, but he was shown no mercy.
- He is flawless in his beauty; even so, he was not considered handsome when he walked here on earth.
- He is the God of truth, and yet they conspired to lie against him.
- He is a God of mercy but was shown no mercy.
- He is the Lord our shepherd, but he was led like a lamb to the slaughter.
- He freely gave his life to the world, but the world without regard for his gift violently took his life.
- He is the rock of our salvation, yet he was crushed for our iniquities.
- He is the author of healing but was bruised and broken.
- He is the author of life who was put to death.
- He is God eternal, and yet his life was ended.
- He is a consuming fire, but his life was snuffed out.
- He was born so that he could die.
- He became a baby so that he could become the King of Kings.
- He humbled himself to be exalted.
- He suffered temptation so that he could be sinless.
- He spoke in puzzles and parables to help us see clearly.
- He was persecuted and bound in order to bring freedom.

- He was torn and bruised to bring healing.
- He was pierced to ease our pain.
- He died to bring life.
- He descended into hell to help us ascend to heaven.
- He left this earth so that he could be with us.
- He forgave us so that he might one day be our judge.

At every juncture he walked out the Father's will for his life by living the paradox. With every step, he went in a direction other than claiming what was rightfully his. With every choice, he modeled submission, service, servanthood, and self-sacrifice. He was radical in his statements, his approach was revolutionary, he was astounding for his insights, people were amazed at his authority when he spoke, and the religious leaders asked, "What manner of teaching is this?" Ultimately, he turned everything they thought they knew about spirituality upside down.

He confounded the "wise" religious leaders of his day because he taught that to become a leader, you must become a servant, to find your life, you must first lose it, and to become great, you must first humble yourself and become meek. He said that if you want eternal life, you must die to self; if you want freedom, you must become a slave to righteousness; and if you want patience and love, you must understand the fellowship of his suffering. If you want to gain power, admit your helplessness. If you want fame, take the lower seat. If you want maturity, become like a little child. If you want joy, you must suffer persecution for his name's sake. Also, to bear much fruit, you must let God radically prune you. To find love, you must give it away, and to receive, you should freely give.

And then, just when the Pharisees, the Sadducees, and even his own disciples were completely turned around by his behavior and his message, Jesus did something even more radical and astounding. Finally, he said, "As the Father has sent me, so send I you" (John 20:21). How did the Father send the Son? In paradox! And now he—in turn and in a very real and practical way—is asking us to live by these challenging paradoxes and to be just like Christ.

Riddle me this: what is the key to everyday practical Christian living? Just like the early disciples did, we learn that we have become servants "by the commission God gave [us] to present to you the Word of God in its fullness—the mystery that has been kept hidden for ages and generations but is now disclosed to the Lord's people. To them, God has chosen to make known among the Gentiles the glorious riches of this mystery, which is Christ in you, the hope of glory" (Colossians 1:25-27). We do so through the power of the Holy Spirit with which we are supposed to live out the paradoxes as well. "Once, having been asked by the Pharisees when the kingdom of God would come, Jesus replied, 'The kingdom of God does not come with your careful observation, nor will people say, "here it is" or "there it is" because the kingdom of God is within you' (Luke 17:20-21). These paradoxes are supposed to be firmly embedded within each of us such that they overwhelm our old nature and flow out into our everyday behavior.

We often try to make spirituality and the Christian walk too difficult. We make it ethereal and other worldly. But Jesus always tried to make it simple and practical. So, he simply says, "At a wedding, take the lower seat (Luke 14:8).

He gave us simple statements about how to live that make all the difference. These are clear statements on how to behave under certain circumstances. Still, they are juxtaposed to our normal, everyday approach to life. Even though simple and straight forward, they require that we flip our natural tendencies and live out a paradox. So, he says, "Take the lower seat."

It is not rocket science. For a bride, a lot of planning goes into her wedding. Anyone who has spent any length of time with a young bride-to-be knows that there is an inordinate amount of planning that goes into her "special day." All the details of the ceremony (who will be invited, where it will occur, how it will be decorated, etc.) must be meticulously planned out. The lists of details are worked out for days or even months. If there is to be a sit-down dinner or reception, the bride gives careful thought to where each guest will be seated. Where is the wedding party, where is the family, where are the friends? These are all important matters that matter greatly to the bride. On her special day of honor, how will she choose to honor her family and friends?

Then suppose you—in arrogance or pride—decide that because of your position in the family or as a friend, you should be sitting at one of the front tables. So, you take your position at a lead table. Now you have ruined her special day. This is because either she or someone else will have to tell you to move so that the person she planned to be in that spot is able to sit there. She feels bad because she had to ask you to move. The person you displaced feels bad because they have now displaced you. Her dream of how this day would go already has one glaring disruption in it because of your choice. It is all just too much painful drama.

If on the other hand you take the lower seat, then if she had other plans, she could honor you by asking you to move forward. Each person may be honored by her as he or she takes the place that has been her dream for this day. Even if you are left at the lower seat, you have still been honored by being asked to be at her wedding.

It is all so simple and practical. The paradoxes that Jesus asks us to live by are just that: simple and practical. Far too often we try to make spirituality complicated and other worldly. So even though it is sometimes difficult in our fallen earthly natures to embrace the paradox, Jesus simply invites us to live the paradox. As such, he tells us to act in ways that don't fit our human inclinations:

- If someone curses you, bless them (Matthew 5:34).
- If compelled, walk the extra mile (Matthew 5:41).
- If wronged, show mercy (Luke 6:36).
- If insulted, rejoice and be glad (Matthew 5:12).
- If your rights are violated, be a peacemaker (Matthew 5:9).
- If you are persecuted, rejoice (Luke 6:23).
- If abused, turn the other cheek (Matthew 5:39).

Even though it is simple, it is not always easy. One summer after returning home from camp, I was excited about the things of God and what I had learned during that experience. In previous years, our youth group had come back from summer camp excited about the lessons learned but all too quickly forgot them as we got back into the normal everyday routine of school. This particular year we—as a youth group under the leadership of a mentor—decided to do something different. We each were tasked with trying to live out the discipleship principles we had been learning at summer camp. Our mentor filled a bowl full of individual Scriptures typed on little slips of paper. Each of us was to blindly pull out one scripture from the bowl and then try to live out that Scripture for the next semester.

Guess which Scripture I pulled out of that bowl. You guessed it; "turn the other cheek." This process of living out the Scripture was further challenged by each of us having an accountability partner to whom we would report back each week on how the process was going.

In thinking about which verse I chose that day, I believe God has a funny sense of humor. I thought okay; how hard can this be? That is, until midweek during the first week of the semester when a big hulk of a guy sat next to me in class and "introduced" himself by pounding his fist as hard as he could into my upper arm. Immediately I knew that this turn-the-other-cheek thing was not going to be a walk in the park. This "introduction" was no small tap on the shoulder. It was the kind of bone jarring hit that left a massive black and blue mark. You know, the kind that after several days turns yellow and green as it tries to dissipate the injury under the surface. However, the bruise never had a chance to turn yellow or green because each day in class my shoulder was freshly "introduced" to my new classmate. I would have given up on turning the other cheek had it not been for our accountability partners.

In our discipleship class, we each discussed our verses and the challenges that we had living them out. My particular story gained a lot of sympathy as the marks of the bruises were so clear on my arm. There was a consensus in the group that I was sitting next to a bully and a real jerk. Even so, the mentor talked to us about how we could still live out kingdom principles even in the face of adversity. So, we kept going with the process.

In a momentary lapse of judgment one day, while trying to live up to this kingdom principle, I asked the classmate if he would like to pound on the other shoulder as well. To my shock and dismay, he did! For the next two weeks straight, I was pounded on both shoulders. Even though the double pounding did not continue past the two weeks, the "introduction" went on all semester.

Finally, two weeks before the end of the semester, the classmate came up to me in the hallway and gave me a massive bear hug. In my mind I thought, "I am dead. I don't know what I've done, but now he's going beyond a punch, and I am going to be killed." Instead, with tears in his eyes the classmate said, "Thank you!" I was taken aback and asked, "What for?" At that point right there in the hallway, he told me his story.

His father was in the military, and they had to move often. At each new school he was picked on as the new kid on the block. Each time as he would just about get settled in, his dad had to move again. So, as he grew and became larger, he decided to be the bully first so that no one would ever pick on him again as the new kid. Obviously, he had had a tough journey.

So that day, in the hall, in front of everyone passing by, and with tears in his eyes, he said, "I just wanted to say thank you. My dad's getting ready to move again, so I will not have another chance to tell you. I just wanted you to know that you are the best friend I have ever had, maybe my only real friend. So, thanks for putting up with me all semester. I am going to miss you."

You see, at a fundamental level and because of our fallen nature, we do not think that these paradoxes work, but they do. Turning the other cheek diffuses the anger, animosity, power, control, or whatever else is going on at the time and opens space for relationship. Relationship is what God our heavenly Father desires for us, and he reminds us of this.

- If someone offends you, take the initiative to go settle the matter and be reconciled (Matthew 5:23).
- If someone is your enemy, love them (Matthew 5:44).
- If someone opposes you, treat them with gentleness (2 Timothy 2:25).
- If you have a great gift to give, do it in secret (Matthew 6:1-3).
- If you are fasting, wash up and look refreshed (Matthew 6:17).
- If you think you deserve something now, delay gratification—possibly even until you get to heaven (Matthew 6:20).
- When it appears as though you have nothing, give away what you do have (Acts 3:6).

So, Peter and John were walking through the gate called beautiful, and a lame man asked for alms. This man had been carried to the gate every day to beg, and now he was looking at Peter and John asking for money. Peter's response is classic. He said, "Look at us." Then the man gave them his attention, expecting to get something from them. Peter said, "Silver or gold I do not have, but what I do have I give you. In the name of Jesus Christ of Nazareth, walk" (Acts 3:5-6). Immediately the lame man was healed, and he rose up and walked.

In fact, Peter had so embraced this paradoxical way of being that there comes a time that even when all that he has to give is his shadow, it is enough. "As a result, people brought the sick into the streets and laid them on beds and mats so that at least Peter's shadow might fall on some of them as he passed by" (Acts 5:15). Jesus' instructions on how to live in paradox are simple and straight forward, and yet their effects are profound.

- If it is important for you to appear knowledgeable, don't be afraid to ask (James 1:5).
- If your situation is impossible, have faith, trust God (Matthew 17:20).
- If someone is spiteful to you, pray for them (Matthew 5:44).
- If you are hungry – go on a fast and seek God (Matthew 6:18).
- If it is important for you to have spiritual understanding, beware of the teachings of religious leaders and be careful to discern their spirit (1 John 4:1).

You may remember your mother saying, "Do not believe everything you see on television." Here we have the Bible version of that same warning. If you are going to live by God's paradoxical principles, you should not believe everything you hear from the pulpit. In God's word, we are instructed to "not believe every spirit but test the spirits to see whether they are from God because many false prophets have gone out into the world" (1 John 4:1). Living by paradox means being "wise as serpents but as harmless as doves" (Matthew 10:16). So, we are presented with even more challenging paradoxes:

- If you want to be forgiven, you must forgive others (Matthew 6:14).
- If you want to be totally free, you must become a slave to righteousness, as defined through paradox (Romans 6:18).
- If you want to follow Christ because you have heard that his burden is light, you must take up your cross and accept your responsibility (Matthew 16:24).
- If you want rest, take his yoke upon you (Matthew 11:29-30).

- If it is important for you, your family, your church, or your nation to appear strong, humble yourself and pray (1 Peter 5:6).
- If you want real spiritual power, let the Holy Spirit lead you through a time of tempting and trial (1 Peter 1:7).

Jesus Christ is our ultimate example, and he very specifically asked John the Baptist to baptize him to allow him to fulfill all righteousness. Even though he was the Son of the living God, as our example he felt it necessary to complete everything that we would need to do to live holy lives. So, then he was led into the wilderness to be tempted of the devil by the Holy Spirit immediately after being baptized and having the Holy Spirit alight on him. Even though we are to pray as Jesus instructed in the Lord's Prayer that he lead us not into temptation; clearly that was the first thing that happened when Jesus started his ministry. It was only after the wilderness experience that Jesus came out of the desert full of the power of God. If Jesus truly is our example, then it seems that we too must overcome the temptations to be full of the power of God in our lives and ministries.

- If you want to have real treasure, sell what you do have and give it to the poor (Mark 10:21).
- If you want to have God's blessing, be thankful for what he has already done (Colossians 3:15).
- If you want your influence to be great, start out small—remember the mustard seed (Mark 4:31).
- If your finances are tight, relax. God will take care of you (Matthew 6:25-34).
- If you want to save your life, you must first lose it (Matthew 10:39).
- If you want to be first, you must be the very last and the servant of all (Mark 9:35).
- If you want to show how mature you are, become like a little child in faith believing (Matthew 18:4).
- If you want to live eternally, die to self now—each and every day (Colossians 3:5).

Ultimately as Christians, we . . .

- . . . are challenged to see unseen things (2 Corinthians 4:18).
- . . . reign by serving (Revelation 5:10).
- . . . become wise by being fools for Christ's sake—at least in the eyes of those who have not yet embraced this relational kingdom (1 Corinthians 1:18).

Jesus' entire life and ministry was spent being true to his nature and modeling these principles of paradoxical living for us. For three years he very pointedly and persistently taught these principles of living. And yet even right up until his death, the disciples still were not "getting it." So, on the night of his betrayal, he stooped to wash the disciples' feet (John 13:5).

The Almighty God, the Everlasting Father,
The King of Kings, the Lord of Lords,
The Prince of Peace, the Master of the Universe,
The Lamb slain from the foundation of the world,
The One before whom all creatures in heaven and in earth will bow low crying Holy, Holy, Holy,
The One who was and is and is to come,
The Alpha and Omega is washing their feet, but *they still did not understand.*

So Peter, viewing Jesus as too important for this task, said, "You shall never wash my feet." Then Jesus answered Peter by saying that this concept is so central, so crucial, and so much a part of what he came to communicate that if Peter didn't let him wash his feet, he would have no part in the kingdom (John 13:8). Yet Peter still did not completely understand. Peter—in his naive eagerness to get it right and show Christ that he is with him—said, "Okay, then wash my whole body." It was as if Jesus had to say, "Peter, it is not about the washing, it is about the paradox of servant leadership." And I believe Jesus would say to us just as he did to his disciples on another occasion, "Have you been with me this long and you still do not know me?" (John 14:9).

It is not about miracles, gifts, signs, and wonders. It is about everyday little choices one after another upending our natural tendencies and fleshing out the paradoxes in each and every circumstance of life. When we do this, the signs will follow. Christ comes into our lives to turn on end everything we think we know about spirituality. And finally, because we live out the paradoxes, we become—as Peter describes—"a chosen people, a royal priesthood, a holy nation, God's special possession, that you may declare the praises of him who called you out of darkness into his wonderful light" (1 Peter 2:9). Only then do we truly become "the salt of the earth" and "the light of the world" (Matthew 5:13-14). This is so that "your light [may] shine before others, that they may see your good deeds and glorify your Father in heaven" (Matthew 5:16).

So, what is the key to everyday practical Christian living? Living a life of paradox. The kingdom life is one that is within you. When you live by the paradoxes, you are manifesting that the kingdom is at hand. However, this can only be true to the extent that you live out the paradoxes of Christ in your everyday life through the power of the Holy Spirit. Only then can we make known "this mystery, which is Christ in you, the hope of glory" (Colossians 1:27). When that does happen, the kingdom truly is within you. Also, when the kingdom is within you, it cannot help but flow out from you to impact others. As Jesus said, "rivers of living water will flow from within them" (John 7:38).

"Do not conform to the pattern of this world but be transformed by the renewing of your mind."

Romans 12:2

18   **Conforming to His Will**

Mysterious Transformation

You are the process by which God is establishing His kingdom. God is painting a picture with your life. You are part of his master plan, part of that intricate tapestry that God is weaving. The challenge that arises, as has been stated before, is that human beings are notorious for getting it wrong and messing things up. In our fallen state, our relationships and behavior are problematic. In fact, as we have seen, entrusting relationship to us is risky and often messy. That being the case, where do we even start to try to live up to the task of establishing the relational kingdom that has been left to us?

We have been given a roadmap to the kingdom life in the parables of Jesus Christ. He has gone out of his way to make plain and clear to us what kingdom living looks like through the paradoxes that he both taught and lived out as examples for us. Also, he has given us the gift of the Holy Spirit to empower us to be able to accomplish our mission. Even so, in our own human frailties, we have a hard time fully embracing the lifestyle that is so necessary if God's purposes in our lives are ever to be fulfilled.

Fortunately, when we accept Jesus as our Savior and believe in his birth, life, death, resurrection, and what it means for us, and when we invite him to be lord of our lives, he promises that "if anyone is in Christ," he is a new creation (2 Corinthians 5:17). God the Father also states that "I will give you a new heart and put a new spirit in you; I will remove from you your heart of stone and give you a heart of flesh. And I will put my Spirit in you and move you to follow my decrees and be careful to keep my laws" (Ezekiel 36:26-27). So, the moment we become a new creation by being "born again"—"children born not of natural descent, nor of human decision or a husband's will, but born of God" (John 1:13)—then the "want to" has been turned around in our lives.

That is all great news. For our old nature with it desires and tendencies is "crucified with Christ" (Galatians 2:20), and we have become a new creation. Even so, what the baby Christian just newly born into the kingdom quickly discovers is that we still wrestle with our old desires, our fallen nature, our previous habits, and all the conditioning of our past life that we can so easily fall back into. Paul explains it this way: "So I find this law at work: Although I want to do good, evil is right there with me. For in my inner being I delight in God's law, but I see another law at work in me, waging war against the law of my mind and making me a prisoner of the law of sin at work within me. What a wretched man I am! Who will rescue me from this body that is subject to death?" (Romans 7:21-24). So even though my "want to" has been changed when I am "born again," there is still a battle that must be fought to overcome the old nature.

In response to Paul's question of "who will do the rescuing?," he says, "Thanks be to God, who delivers me through Jesus Christ our Lord" (Romans 7:25). He also goes on to say that "those who live according to the flesh have their minds set on what the flesh desires; but those who live in accordance with the Spirit have their minds set on what the Spirit desires. The mind governed by the flesh is death, but the mind governed by the spirit is life and peace" (Romans 8:5-6). And it is here that we begin to see where the real battle is. It is in our minds.

Therefore, if we are the process by which the kingdom is established, we are going to have to begin the process of stepping up to the task at hand by focusing intently on the battle for our mind. The way we think, the things that get our attention, the beliefs we hold, and the subsequent choices we make all need to be reshaped in order to fall in line with a kingdom mindset. Paul again says, "Therefore, I urge you, brothers and sisters, in view of God's mercy, to offer your bodies a living sacrifice, holy and pleasing to God—this is your true and proper worship. Do not conform to the pattern of this world, but be transformed by the renewing of your mind" (Romans 12:1-2).

We are challenged to grow with ever increasing glory into the image of Christ (2 Corinthians 3:18). If this relational kingdom is ever going to be built, then "in your relationships with one another, have the same mindset as Jesus Christ" (Philippians 2:5). But how do we develop this attitude, this nature, this mindset—especially since it is so radically different than our own previous fallen human nature?

Here is where the real challenge lies. Fundamentally the human mind is an associative process. By that I mean that across our entire lifespan, the job of the human brain has been to make associations—connections between sights, sounds, tastes, smells, touch, movement, and stimuli from the environment. Early on in development, these associations focus primarily on our senses and movement. If you ever watch a newborn baby, you can track the connections being made in real time. With the early development of eye-hand coordination, you can see the absolute delight in a child's face as their hand finally connects with the mobile above them in their crib.

Later in life the associations become much more complex as we learn how our behavior affects others, what works and does not work, how to process what we think and what others think of us, as well as many other complex human interactions. In our fallen world, actions, reactions, posturing, pride, lusts, envy, jealousy, and many other sometimes problematic and intricate relational processes are learned by our interactions with others. All this learning is facilitated by associations or connections that are made in the brain. What we think and ultimately how we behave is all mediated by the associations we have built up over a lifetime. So how we behave is mediated by what we think in our mind, what we think in our minds is mediated by the associations we have generated from experience, and those associations are often triggered by stimuli in the environment.

It is this lifetime of associations that must be deconstructed and our minds renewed if we are ever going to be able to live out the kingdom paradoxes and follow the roadmap of the parables of Jesus Christ. Both the parables and the paradoxes require us to flip on end our natural tendencies and live by a very different mindset. If we are ever going to be able to accomplish this, we must be proactive about how and what we think instead of just reacting based on experience. You are to "put off your old self, which is being corrupted by its deceitful desires, to be made new in the attitudes of your minds, and to put on the new self" (Ephesians 4:22-24). We need to change our mind about how we respond to the triggers that have been conditioned from our past.

But how do we effectively fight this battle between our old nature and the new creation that we have become? How do we deconstruct the old ways of thinking and reacting? How to we successfully overcome our problematic thought processes that have been so strongly shaped by a fallen world view. The answer is "Christ in you, the hope of glory" (Colossian 1:27). We cannot do this by ourselves. Fortunately, this is a relational kingdom, and the king desperately wants to work with you and in you to help you be successful. There is a mysterious transformation that must take place. Here is what his Word says:

> Be strong in the Lord and in his mighty power. Put on the full armor of God, so that you can take your stand against the devil's schemes. For our struggle is not against flesh and blood, but against the rulers, against the authorities, against the powers of this dark world and against the spiritual forces of evil in the heavenly realms.
>
> Therefore, put on the full armor of God so that when the day of evil comes, you may be able to stand your ground, and after you have done everything, to stand. Stand firm then, with the belt of truth buckled around your waist, with the breastplate of righteousness in place, and with your feet fitted with the readiness that comes from the gospel of peace. In addition to all this, take up the shield of faith, with which you can extinguish all the flaming arrows of the evil one. Take the helmet of salvation and the sword of the Spirit, which is the word of God. (Ephesians 6:10-17)

Notice that the author states that our battle is not against flesh and blood. Unfortunately, far too often we end up fighting all the wrong battles against flesh and blood. We are not to be fighting ourselves and our own behavior because Christ has already made the ultimate sacrifice to atone for our sins. We should not be fighting other Christians over doctrinal beliefs. Remember that Jesus Christ's prayer is that we would be unified. We should not be fighting as Christians against unbelievers. We will not win them over by our apologetics and condemnation. Instead, the Bible is clear that we will win them over by our love. We should not be engaged in culture wars and fighting to legislate morality through politics. These are all flesh and blood struggles that are a misdirection of our energy.

Instead, we should be directing our efforts against the true enemies. To do so, we need special weapons, ". . . not the weapons of the world. On the contrary, they have divine power to demolish strongholds" (2 Corinthians 10:4). This armor of God—the weapons we use and the battle we engage in—should be directed at Satan, his fiery darts, and the other dark forces of this world. But how do we do that? How do we know what those dark forces are doing? Fortunately,

God—through his word—has clarified what the strongholds are and what the enemy is about. God does so by stating that "We demolish arguments and every pretension that sets itself up against the knowledge of God, and we take captive every thought to make it obedient to Christ" (2 Corinthians 10:5). The battlefield is our mind: what we think, what we believe, the things that get our attention, and the choices we make as a result.

The King James Version of the Bible says, "As a man thinks in his heart, so is he" (Proverbs 23:7). So, it matters greatly how we think and what we attend to. This is where the real battle is taking place. The spiritual rulers, authorities, and all other forces of evil are targeting your thought life. Their desire is to have you focus your thoughts, energies, and time on anything other than Jesus Christ and his kingdom. When we live like the rest of the world with our thoughts consumed by earthly things, then we lose the battles. Instead, we are asked to "set [our] minds on things above, not on earthly things" (Colossians 3:2). When we do so, God "will keep in perfect peace those whose minds are steadfast because they trust in [God]" (Isaiah 26:3).

Therefore, the real challenge across our lifespan is discovering how to "take captive every thought to make it obedient to Christ" (2 Corinthians 10:5). As you may recall, part of the Great Commission states that we should be taught to observe all things whatsoever he has commanded us (Matthew 28:20). If Jesus Christ is the true king of this mysterious kingdom of heaven, then what Jesus commands should be followed by his subjects. Unfortunately, as Paul has so eloquently described, our old nature is at war with the new creation in the battlefield of our mind. Also, since there are evil principalities, malicious authorities, and strong powers of darkness that are vying for our thoughts and attention, the battle is not an easy one nor is it a battle that will just automatically be won.

The world we live in has many forces that are insidiously trying to capture our minds. The cares of life, worldly desires, negative interpersonal interactions, desperate reactions to life's circumstances, cultural norms, countercultural revolutions that push conventional boundaries, sexual immorality, non-modest fashion trends, the media's influence through television and movies, and social media's often provocative and reactionary posts all invite us to think in ways that are counterproductive to the kingdom of heaven's more helpful mindset. The forces are so many and so thoroughly interwoven throughout our society that on our own we could never hope to overcome them. But, as has already been stated, the answer is tied up in the mystery of Christ in you, which is the hope of glory. Since this new kingdom we are part of is fundamentally a relational process, we must rely on our relationship with the King. That is why you will hear in many Christian settings that this process is not about religion; it is about relationship. If you are ever going to be victorious in the battle for your mind, it will be so only to the extent that you allow Christ to reign in you freely. As a result, Paul states that we who share in this heavenly calling should "fix our thoughts on Jesus, whom we acknowledge as our apostle and high priest" (Hebrews 3:1).

For this to happen, Paul has stated that "I die daily" (1 Corinthians 15:31). He goes on to say, "For we know that our old self was crucified with him so that the body ruled by sin might be done away with, that we should no longer be slaves to sin" (Romans 6:6). In becoming a new creation in Christ, he states that "I have been crucified with Christ and I no longer live, but Christ lives in me" (Galatians 2:20). As such, if we ever hope to win the battle of the mind, if we really desire this mysterious transformation to occur, we also need to embrace this idea of dying to self each and every day so that Christ may live in and through us. This is clearly another one of the mysterious paradoxes that are part of kingdom living. We live in a human body with all its flaws and frailty and yet to the degree that we will fully embrace it, we live with the mind of Christ.

If you will commit to doing this, then you will start focusing on "whatever is true, whatever is noble, whatever is right, whatever is pure, whatever is lovely, whatever is admirable—if anything is excellent or praiseworthy—think about such things" (Philippians 4:8). Then, as you embrace this way of thinking, "whatever you have learned or received or heard from [Paul] , or seen in [Paul] put it into practice" (Philippians 4:9). As you do so your focus and filter will increasingly be through God's Word and through the Holy Spirit rather than the lens of your own past experience, your woundedness, your preferences, or your or other's opinions. This fundamental shift in processing is something you must be intentional about every day. The culture around you will resist this new way of thinking and therefore you must be all the more diligent to shape the way you think. Then, as you partner with the King of this relational kingdom, amazing things will begin to happen around you. Significantly, what also happens in this partnership toward a mysterious transformation of the mind is that God has promised that "he who began a good work in you will carry it on to completion" (Philippians 1:6). The battle for your mind is not yours alone. He has promised to help you every step along the way.

"For this very reason, make every effort to add to your faith goodness; and to goodness, knowledge; and to knowledge, self-control; and to self-control, perseverance; and to perseverance, godliness; and to godliness, brotherly kindness; and to brotherly kindness, love."

2 Peter 1:5-7

The Eight Essentials

Secret Solutions

As we enter this new kind of relational kingdom, we find ourselves up against a paradox. We are born again into a relational kingdom that we—by ourselves—are ill equipped to handle. Even as we begin the process of renewing our minds in partnership with the Holy Spirit, we find ourselves as infants in a world of turmoil that can only effectively be handled by extremely mature Christians. As we have stated before, what is truly necessary is a developmental model for Christian maturity.

In recognizing this dilemma, Peter states that "like newborn babies, [you should] crave pure spiritual milk, so that by it you may grow up in your salvation" (1 Peter 2:2). He clearly recognizes that we are going to need to grow up quickly to be able to handle the tasks ahead of us. Paul goes on to say that we need to move even beyond that, such that "anyone who lives on milk, being still an infant, is not acquainted with the teaching about righteousness. But solid food is for the mature, who by constant use have trained themselves to distinguish good from evil" (Hebrews 5:13-14). So, both Peter and Paul stress that we need to grow up and mature to effectively navigate this new kingdom life that we have been born into. As such, Paul states, "Therefore, let us move beyond the elementary teachings about Christ and be taken forward to maturity, not laying again the foundation of repentance from acts that lead to death, and of faith in God, instructions about cleansing rites, the laying on of hands, the resurrection of the dead, and eternal judgment" (Hebrews 6:1-2).

Interestingly enough, these are many of the fundamental doctrines of most of the major Christian denominations. We far too often feel as though if a person believes all these, then they are a strong Christian. But wait a minute; this is simply what you believe. When you believe, you become born again. Great, that is your new birth into the kingdom as an infant. Paul pleads with us to move beyond these elementary teachings about Christ and to become mature Christians. But how do we do so?

Yet Another Paradox

Jesus lived out a perfect example of mature Christianity through the paradoxes he modeled in his own life. He also taught the principles of mature Christian living through the parables that he consistently shared with his disciples. Finally, he ascended to heaven and then sent the Holy Spirit to bring all these things to our remembrance and to empower us to be able to accomplish this process of spiritual development and maturity. But then, through his word in the writings of Paul, he turns around and says to "work out your own salvation with fear and trembling" (Philippians 2:12).

And here is where the real challenge lies. We are in a relational kingdom where God has done his part. God, the Father, orchestrated everything in heaven and earth to point to redemption and make this kingdom possible. Then Jesus the son sacrificed his own life and taught us how this kingdom could be possible. Next the Holy Spirit came to empower us to take on the task left to us. But because this is a relational kingdom, we too are given a part. Our part is to work out our own salvation, to mature as Christians, and then to become the process by which the kingdom is established. And just in case you might feel overwhelmed by that prospect, he promises that "his divine power has given us everything we need for a godly life through our knowledge of him who called us by his own glory and goodness" (2 Peter 1:3).

So, if he has given us everything that pertains to life and godliness, then why do so many young Christians feel so inadequate and ill equipped? Here is where we begin to see the true nature of the relational kingdom we were born into. Perhaps the reason we so often feel inadequate is that we try to go it alone. We too often make this about a "personal" relationship with God. Instead, "we were all baptized by one Spirit so as to form one body" (1 Corinthian 12:13). Perhaps some of the everything you need resides in those fellow believers around you. That is why his Word says, "forsake not the assembling of yourselves together" (Hebrew 10:25). His Word also states that "as iron sharpens iron, so one person sharpens another" (Proverbs 27:17). As new Christians, we are operating in a kingdom whose ground rules are different than this world's ground rules. Instead of pulling ourselves up by our own bootstraps, we either grow together or we do not grow very well at all. Furthermore, because we are now functioning in a relational kingdom, we need to grow up quickly in our knowledge of what makes relationships work.

Peter's Commission

In his writings to the Early Church, Peter clearly understood this need for a developmental model of Christian maturity, and he placed an extraordinarily significant amount of energy into helping with that much needed instruction. But to get a feel for the enormity of what he was trying to do, we need to step back a bit in his personal journey. If you recall, there was a time when he had denied Jesus three times. This had been foretold by Jesus. Peter had promised that it would never happen, and yet Peter finds himself doing just that before the rooster crowed the next morning. Devastated, Peter is overwhelmed by his own behavior. So, it is with great difficulty when he finally realizes that Jesus is alive and runs to the shore to reconnect with his master, that he reengages only to hear Jesus ask, "Peter, do you love me?" (John 21:15-17). It must have cut Peter to the core to hear his Lord and Master ask such a question. His immediate response was to say, "Lord, you know that I do." When he does, Jesus says, "Feed my sheep." But then imagine Peter's overwhelming sense of concern when Jesus asks the same question two more times. Peter again reaffirms his commitment to Christ, and each time Jesus says, "feed my sheep." So then, this becomes Peter's life mission. He does everything in his power from that day forward to equip the saints for the task at hand, to feed the sheep that so desperately need to mature in order to live the kingdom life.

It is with this as background that we come to the end of Peter's life, to a time when he will soon be crucified for the sake of the kingdom. He has spent his entire ministry trying to live up to the commission that Jesus had given Peter: to feed his sheep. Now he has but one chance left to drive home the enormity of the lessons that he had so diligently tried to pass on to Christ's followers. As such, he says, "So I will always remind you of these things even though you know them and are firmly established in the truth you now have. I think it is right to refresh your memory as long as I live in the tent of this body because I know that I will soon put it aside, as our Lord Jesus Christ has made clear to me. And I will make every effort to see that after my departure you will always be able to remember these things" (2 Peter 1:12-15).

What we have here is a deathbed confession. Typically, we add extra weight to the words of a man who knows he is going to die. Of all the things he could possibly say, Peter stresses that this is the most important. So, he says, "For this very reason, make every effort to add to your (1) faith, (2) goodness; and to goodness, (3) knowledge; and to knowledge, (4) self-control; and to self-control, (5) perseverance; and to perseverance, (6) godliness; and to godliness, (7) brotherly kindness; and to brotherly kindness, (8) love" (2 Peter 1:5-7). And here in these few short words Peter lays out a lifetime of spiritual ministry. He presents a developmental growth model that sums up all the feeding of sheep that he has done during his life.

He then says, "For if you possess these qualities in increasing measure, they will keep you from being ineffective and unproductive in your knowledge of our Lord Jesus Christ. But whoever does not have them is nearsighted and blind, forgetting that they have been cleansed from their past sins. Therefore, my brothers and sisters, make every effort to confirm your calling and election. For if you do these things, you will never stumble, and you will receive a rich welcome into the eternal kingdom of our Lord and Savior Jesus Christ" (2 Peter 1:8-11).

So now we not only have a deathbed confession, but we also have been given a fool proof guarantee. In these eight steps, we are given a developmental model where step by step we are told what to add next. In addition, it is a growth model because we are told to possess these things in increasing measure. In other words, we are never done growing but keep increasing in each of these areas. After all we are growing from glory to glory into the image of Christ.

But how can the core of the kingdom life be described in just eight steps, eight simple concepts that equip us with everything we need? Far too often we quickly gloss over these eight steps and fail to see their importance. Even though Peter lays them out for us clearly, they often remain as secret solutions because they are not known or seen as the keys to maturity. For too many in contemporary Christianity these are nice virtues that might be great to have but they are not a priority. Peter declared that these are the keys to never stumbling and having a rich welcome into the eternal kingdom of our Lord and Savior Jesus Christ. Unfortunately, all too often, just like the old Book of Virtues that would sit on our coffee tables as nice words on a page, these concepts are hardly ever opened and applied to our lives.

Worse yet, we may not even see them as nice words. Instead, we may almost immediately dismiss these concepts by saying things like, "I'm sorry; I am not a patient person. That is just not my personality." If you have ever found yourself in that camp, notice that these are not like the gifts of the spirit or the different ministries where God distributes them as he wills: to one this gift and to another that ministry. No, we are all required to have all of these qualities. In fact, Peter states that if anyone does not have them, "he is nearsighted and blind, and has forgotten that he has been cleansed from his past sins" (2 Peter 1:9).

With these eight concepts, Peter has given us the secret solutions to a kingdom life. He has clearly laid out the principles that make relationships work. He fulfills his commission from Jesus Christ to feed his sheep by passing on the core of what it means to be a Christian. Instead of reacting to others the way the world operates, he has given us a model of spiritual development that proactively shows us how to approach and build relationships. So, for a few minutes, let's dive more deeply into that developmental model.

The Developmental Model for Spiritual Maturity

When you look at most developmental models, they usually fall into stages, each one building on the previous. With that in mind, let us examine the eight-step model that Peter presents by paying close attention to the order of development and why each step falls next in the process.

Faith

So why start with faith in this eight-step developmental model? There are several strong reasons for beginning here. First God's word states that "Everyone has been given a measure of faith" (Romans 12:3). Even the most avowed atheist believes something about God. That is where we all start. Even though the measure of faith we each start with may be different, we all have been given some measure of faith. Faith is what we believe, what we hope for, what we aspire to even if it is not yet a reality.

Not only is everyone given a measure of faith, but for those who dare to embrace the kingdom of heaven, the Bible states that "If you declare with your mouth, 'Jesus is Lord,' and believe in your heart that God raised him from the dead, you will be saved" (Romans 10:9).

185

In other words, when you have faith and believe in Jesus Christ, then you are born again into the kingdom of God. When that happens "by grace you have been saved through faith and this is not from yourselves; it is the gift of God (Ephesians 2:8). This ultimately is the starting point in the kingdom for everyone. Having faith, believing in God, is how we start off in this relational kingdom that is at hand.

On one occasion a jailer asked Paul what he should do to be saved. Paul replied, "Believe in the Lord Jesus, and you will be saved" (Acts 16:31). In fact, "without faith, it is impossible to please God because anyone who comes to him must believe that he exists and that he rewards those who earnestly seek him" (Hebrews 11:6). But once we do believe and have faith, we are born-again. We become alive in the spirit or, in other words, we become spiritual babies. Then, to grow into mature Christians, we need to increase in faith. There is always room to have more faith. In fact, Jesus encouraged us to increase in faith on multiple occasions. He was also often lamenting that so many of his would-be followers had so little faith. So, Peter teaches us that we should possess these things in increasing measure. But faith, even though it is powerful and can move mountains, by itself is not enough. Therefore, Peter encourages us to add the other steps as well.

Goodness

Peter says to add goodness to your faith. While goodness might be considered a character trait by some, more often than not it is an action-oriented step. In fact, when speaking of Jesus, the Bible states that "he went around doing good" (Act 10:38). The only way we know that someone is good is by what they do. Most often it is by what is done for others that a person's character is defined, which is why James states, "What good is it, my brothers and sisters, if someone claims to have faith but has no deeds?" (James 2:13). He goes on in a very clear manner to say that "faith by itself, if it is not accompanied by action, is dead" (James 2:17).

For example, if I tell you that I believe a chair is structurally sound and will hold my weight, you might state that I have faith in the chair. However, what would happen if every time I approach the chair instead of sitting firmly down in the chair, I hovered two inches over it in a semi-seated position? Not only would I get very fatigued from holding that position, but anyone watching me would not believe that I had faith that the chair would hold me. Until I take the decisive step

186

to sit firmly in the chair, my "faith" in the chair is in effect dead.

In the same way, many people claim to have faith in God. Even so, all the while they try to accomplish everything on their own and become quickly overwhelmed and fatigued. It is not until we see that faith in action as a person intentionally partners with Jesus Christ and sets about doing good for others that we really know they believe in God. This relational kingdom requires that we partner with God and that we demonstrate the love that his disciples will be known by. But love, like faith, is only truly manifested when it results in action toward others that is to their benefit. Ultimately, to have goodness as a character trait, it somehow must be demonstrated in personal action. This is true not just once or twice by an occasional good deed but must be an ongoing process, which is why Peter stressed that we should possess this trait as well in increasing measure.

Knowledge

Add knowledge to your goodness. This next step of being informed by knowledge is essential in the development of Christian maturity. Far too often there are well-meaning young Christians who believe God and are trying to do something with their faith, but who are, unfortunately, very much like a bull in a china shop. By this I mean that they are wreaking havoc everywhere they go. Even though they are well intentioned, their lack of knowledge concerning the things of God gets them in trouble. That is why in the Amplified Bible you are told to "study and do your best to present yourself to God approved, a workman [tested by trial] who has no reason to be ashamed, accurately handling and skillfully teaching the word of truth" (2 Timothy 2:15).

If we are ever to mature as Christians, we dare not remain Biblically illiterate. Just as a young child needs a healthy diet to grow and mature physically, a young Christian needs to be consuming the word of God to grow and mature spiritually. Since we are growing up in a different kind of kingdom, we need to understand the nature and principles of that kingdom. Otherwise, our actions will not serve the kingdom well. Far too often, action without knowledge is counterproductive.

To be more effective in his walk with God, David in the Old Testament asked God to "Teach [him] good judgement and knowledge" (Psalm 119:66). Later David's son, Solomon, asked for wisdom from God. Because God saw that request as extremely beneficial both for Solomon and for the nation of Israel, he also promised to bless Solomon with wealth and honor. In the New Testament, Peter encourages us to "grow in the grace and knowledge of our Lord and Savior Jesus Christ" (2 Peter 3:18). Paul also stresses growing in the knowledge of the Lord and of his will (Colossians 1:9). One of the Proverbs says, "Let the wise hear and increase in learning, and let the one who understands obtain guidance" (Proverbs1:5). It is this guidance that is necessary if a young Christian is ever going to be able to act on their faith in a mature way that becomes productive rather than counterproductive. Therefore, "an intelligent heart acquires knowledge, and the ear of the wise seeks knowledge" (Proverbs 18:15). Once again, Peter stresses that we should possess knowledge in an ever-increasing measure. In other words, in this new relational kingdom, we should become lifelong learners.

Self-Control
Add self-control to your knowledge. We live in a fallen world that far too often invites us to live reactive lives. If we are ever going to break away from that level of disfunction and live more proactive lives, then we are desperately going to need to be able to exercise self-control. Even if I have faith in God, I am trying to do something about it, and I have been in church or in my own personal devotions long enough to have a reasonable level of knowledge concerning the things of the kingdom of heaven; if I do not have self-control, that knowledge will not help me. For the newfound knowledge of the kingdom to be effective in my life, I must exercise personal discipline to implement the knowledge I now have. Self-control is the step that allows the theoretical knowledge acquired to become a practical reality in my everyday behavior.

If I am ever going to be able to live out the paradoxes that are part of my Christian heritage and identity as a child of God, then I must exercise a lot of self-control. After all, as we have said before, even though turning the other cheek is a very simple and straight forward thing to do, it is not always an easy thing to do. This is particularly true in the heat of the moment when our old fallen nature screams at us to just react. One of the significant challenges of this era is that far too many Christian believers fall into the same patterns that the rest of their surrounding culture does. For example, our current culture encourages us to want immediate results, to be impatient when that is not forthcoming, and to be reactionary with our responses as a result. Unfortunately, that kind of living is entirely too much like an infant's behavior. If we are to mature, then self-control, delayed gratification, proactive behavior, and temperance are necessary skills we must develop. Living the paradox or flipping our natural tendencies on end requires a great deal of self-control, and this too we should possess in increasing measure.

Perseverance

Add perseverance to your self-control. Almost anyone can exercise a little self-control when they are getting a lot of praise or pats on the back. It is easy to be self-controlled when the circumstances are all positive and the challenges are few. But what happens when circumstances become difficult? What kind of self-control does it take to keep going even when no one else notices? What if the challenges are many? What if the proactive way of living a kingdom life requires that I exhibit self-control over the long haul even when there is no immediate payoff. What if it means delaying gratification for some more noble purpose? This is where perseverance becomes critical. We should "not become weary in doing good, for at the proper time we will reap a harvest if we do not give up" (Galatians 6:9).

Christ's disciples and apostles have all addressed these secret solutions for growth and maturity. They each use their own words, but they are all talking about the same steps. One calls this particular step "patience"; another calls it "endurance." Still others call it "perseverance," "long-suffering," "persistence," "wearying not in well doing," "carrying on," "fainting not," "standing fast," "not giving up," "being steadfast," or even "forbearance." Whatever the term used, each of the many Christ followers stressed the importance of these developmental steps to Christian maturity. Hanging in there when it is difficult, when there is no immediate payoff, and particularly when no one notices is an essential component of the mature Christian life. Even Jesus said, "In this world you will have trouble. But take heart for I have overcome the world" (John16:33). There will be times when things are difficult and that is when we most need to persevere. And yes, even this perseverance is something that we should possess in increasing measure throughout our lives.

Godliness

Add godliness to your perseverance. Of these eight essential elements, perhaps the most misunderstood is this one. Far too often godliness is confused with the old "holiness" preaching. By this I do not mean the verses in the Bible that ask us to be holy because God is holy (1 Peter 1:16; Leviticus 19:2). Instead, I am referring to the all-too-often-preached, gender-biased sermons that focus on women's makeup, attire, modesty, and behavior. While the scriptures do talk about the importance of believers setting a good example through their choices and behavior, that is not what it means to be godly. Also, when addressing our behavior and attire, the Scriptures are clear that what adorns the heart on the inside of a man or of a woman is far more important than what is on the outside. Even though holiness is one of God's attributes, just how we appear or behave is still not what it means to be godly.

If we really want to know what it means to be like God as we come to this next developmental step, we should look at the life of Jesus Christ. After all, Jesus said, "Anyone who has seen me has seen the Father" (John 14:9). So, let's explore his word to find those times when Jesus was believing his Father, acting on his faith, using his knowledge, exhibiting self-control, and persevering. What does Jesus look like during those times? If we can see that, then we will know what it means to be God-like or to have godliness.

There was a time when Jesus and the disciples got in a boat to cross over to the other side of the Sea of Galilee. As they were in the process of crossing, a great storm came upon them such that the disciples were afraid for their lives. Imagine the enormity of the storm if even seasoned fishermen were afraid for their lives. The windstorm was so strong that "a fierce squall came up, and the waves broke over the boat, so that it was nearly swamped" (Mark 4:37). Where was Jesus? Asleep in the stern of the boat. Even in this dire circumstance, what was it like to be godly? Jesus was perfectly at peace, sound asleep. In fact, peace was so much a part of his godly nature that when he arose, he said, "peace be still," and the whole universe joined him in that moment, and the waves were immediately calmed. Godliness is when you are persevering in a difficult circumstance and are still able to be at peace. In fact, it is a peace that "transcends all understanding" (Philippians 4:7).

On another occasion, Jesus was hanging on a cross, enduring the pain, persevering through one of the most horrific deaths known to man. The weight of the world's sin for all time was placed on his shoulders. The loss of communion with his heavenly Father was even more overwhelming as he cried, "My God, my God, why have you forsaken me" (Matthew 27:46). What does it mean to be God-like in that moment? It says that "For the joy set before him, he endured the cross" (Hebrews 12:2). To be God-like, to have godliness, means having joy in the middle of difficult circumstances because you are able to take the long view and see the positive outcome from your perseverance. That is why James says, "consider it pure joy, my brothers and sisters, whenever you face trials of many kinds because you know that the testing of your faith produces perseverance. Let perseverance finish its work that you may be mature and complete, not lacking anything" (James 1:2-4).

When God created Adam and Eve in the garden, he knew ahead of time that they would eat the apple and bring sin into the world. Even though he foresaw this, he still said that his creation was "very good" (Genesis 1:31). How was he able to do so? By looking ahead to redemption, the kingdom, and in particular your part in the process of establishing his kingdom. He knew then that—by looking into the future—he would be madly in love with you and was looking forward to you not only returning that love but also passing it on to others. Because of this knowledge, he was both at peace and looking forward in time with joyful expectation to the ongoing development of this relational kingdom. All of this in God's mind was very good.

When life throws the inevitable at you and you still choose by faith to persevere, you must do so while embracing the peace that only comes from God. Additionally, you must acknowledge the joy of knowing that your momentary circumstances are working out something far greater in you. After all in the Amplified Version we read, "that God causes all things to work together for good for those who love God, to those who are called according to his plan and purpose" (Romans 8:28). This kind of godliness, is an essential step in developmental maturity that allows you to have joy and peace even in the middle of very difficult and trying circumstances. In other words, we are able to take the long view even if the reward for our current suffering is not given to us until we see Christ in eternity. Ultimately the question is, in the meantime, can we find a way to enjoy the process? The reason this step is so important developmentally is that most people will not persist in something if they cannot find a way to enjoy it and be at peace with it at some level. And yes, once again, we are admonished to increase in godliness.

Brotherly Kindness

Add brotherly kindness to godliness. When you reach this level of maturity, you are pretty much past self. As a result, when you reach out to help others, it is from an abundance of overflow that the rivers of living water come up out of you. Then you truly are helpful to others. This is not at all like the early attempts made back in the goodness phase. Instead, you have now become informed and knowledgeable through your study of God's Word, you have exerted the ongoing self-control that allows you to live out the knowledge you have acquired, you have stuck with it and persevered, and you have found a way to look to the future and therefore enjoy the process of becoming. When you do this, you no longer are overreactive to either circumstances or people. Instead, you set about helping others in a proactive way, living out the kingdom principles that you have learned from the puzzles, parables, and paradoxes. As you reach out to others in this way, you truly do become the salt of the earth and the light of the world. As you are kind to others, you demonstrate the life and actions of Christ. Because you live out the mystery of Christ in you who is the hope of glory, as you share his way of being with others you also bring hope and life to them, this is how the kingdom grows. And once again, you are to be ever increasing in brotherly kindness as well.

Love

And finally, add love to your brotherly kindness. We all know the verse in 1 Corinthians that says, "And now these three remain: faith, hope, and love. But the greatest of these is love" (1 Corinthians 13:13). At the apex of this spiritual developmental process is love. It is the greatest step of spiritual maturity. When we study the attributes of God, the Bible does not say that he works at love, that he does love, or even that he tries to love. Not at all. Instead, it states clearly that God is love (1 John 4:8).

Therefore, as we mature in Christ, we reach a place in our spiritual development when we no longer must work at these concepts and principles. We should practice these spiritual disciplines until they just simply become second nature. Ultimately it is just who we are. That is why Jesus can ask us to love our enemies (Matthew 5:44). We love our enemies not because they do or don't deserve it or even just because we do or don't feel like it. No, instead we love them because it is so much a part of our new nature that we would not consider doing anything else. When that happens, we truly are mature Christians. But even this kind of love must be sought continually. We are ever and always a work in progress. Spiritual maturity is not an end point or a destination. Instead, it is an ongoing process.

In that process, these eight steps are the essential elements for living a godly life. They are the secret solutions to spiritual maturity. If we are ever going to be successful in growing from glory to glory into the image of Christ, we must seek to possess these eight items in increasing measure. The reason that Peter can so confidently state that if we do, we will never fall and we will have an abundant entrance into heaven is that the more we possess these eight essential elements, the more we become like Jesus Christ.

"Pray also for me, that whenever I open my mouth, words may be given me so that I will fearlessly make known the mystery of the gospel."

Ephesians 6:19

Undercover Christian No More

As stated before, God wants us to "grow from glory to glory into the image of Christ" (2 Corinthian 3:18). For this to be effective, we must fully embrace a lifestyle of change. So, God invites us on the journey of renewing our mind and then adding the eight developmental steps of Christian maturity that we have discussed. As we grow in Christ and become more mature, he wants us to **change our minds** and be transformed by that renewal process (Romans 12:2). He invites us to **change our hearts** by declaring, "I will give you a new heart, and a new spirit I will put within you (Ezekiel 36:26). He longs for us to **change our views** so that "they might see with their eyes; hear with their ears; understand with their hearts" (Matthew 13:14). He wants us to **change our focus** so "that the eyes of your heart may be enlightened in order that you may know the hope to which he has called you" (Ephesians 1:18). Through the power of the Holy Spirit, he empowers us to **change our perceptions** so that we perceive more (i.e., the spiritual) than just the natural. Then, like Christ, through the gifts of the Spirit we can perceive when virtue goes out of us (Luke 8:46) or we are able to perceive what others are thinking when it will help to further the kingdom (Luke 5:22). Furthermore, he desires to **change our reactions** so that we can live the paradoxes such as turning the other cheek or walking the extra mile (Matthew 5:38-41). More than anything, he prays for us to **change our relationships** so that we may "grow in unity and in love" (John 17:21). As a critical part of this relational kingdom, he also asks us to **change our mission** and to develop an overwhelming excitement about sharing the kingdom with those around us.

As a result of all these changes and right along with this newly developed spiritual maturity comes a holy boldness. We are compelled to no longer be undercover Christians. We then, just like Paul, can say, "for I am not ashamed of the gospel because it is the power of God that brings salvation to everyone who believes" (Romans 1:16). As we boldly move forward in this kingdom, we realize "the Spirit God gave us does not make us timid, but gives us power, love, and self-discipline" (2 Timothy 1:7). Inevitably we are compelled: "We must proclaim the good news of the kingdom of God" (Luke 4:43).

All this personal growth and dynamic change in our lives does more than just change our words and our testimony. Yes, we do proclaim the good news, but right alongside of that, we live a dynamically different lifestyle. As we grow from glory to glory, more and more into the image of Christ, we also take on a lifestyle that matches our words and powerfully demonstrates the love of the kingdom of God. This newly developed maturity and this newfound lifestyle compel us to embrace some of the more challenging concepts of the Christian journey in that they require personal sacrifice, taking up the cross and following Christ—or in other words—dying to self.

So, what are the challenging concepts that I am referring to? They are obedience, servanthood, and submission. These are the concepts that require true commitment and are also the things most likely to demonstrate true allegiance to the kingdom.

The Issue of Obedience

As discussed earlier, the true battlefield is your mind. Therefore, right now in your mind, Satan is probably telling you that all this build-up just to talk about obedience is overrated. He is most likely inviting you to turn your thoughts elsewhere this very moment. But if you truly love God and desire to have a dynamic part in this relational kingdom, you must embrace another of the many paradoxes that are part of the mystery of Christ in you. Where is the paradox? What is the mystery? The paradox is this: the only true freedom that you will ever find in this life is to become a slave to obedience. Paul states that either "you are slaves to sin, which leads to death, or to obedience, which leads to righteousness" (Romans 6:16). The mystery is that obedience is the path to righteousness, power, and greatness in the kingdom of heaven. In fact, even Jesus—"son though he was, he learned obedience from what he suffered" (Hebrews 5:8). Obedience is not an option; it is an absolute necessity for unity in the body of Christ to occur.

Jesus further elaborates on this principle by saying that "If you keep my commands, you will remain in my love, just as I have kept my Father's commands and remain in his love" (John 15:10). The real question here is do you want to remain in God's love? Do you really love God? Jesus clearly states that "If you love me, you will keep my commands" (John 14:15). John also says that "this is love: that we walk in obedience to his commands" (2 John 1:6). Yet again in another passage John states that "in fact, this is love for God: to keep his commands" (1 John 5:3).

God, through his word, cannot be clearer or more specific. But it is a message we are often reluctant to hear, so much so that we tend to forget that obedience is a significant part of the great commission. We fully embrace the part about going into all the world. Then we somehow limit it to making converts. However, the rest of the great commission states that we should "therefore go and make disciples of all nations, baptizing them in the name of the Father and of the Son and of the Holy Spirit and teaching them to obey everything I have commanded you" (Matthew 28:20).

Did Jesus really sneak that last part in there? You see, you can live a comfortable "Christian" life through sacrifice. You can sacrifice your time by going to church on Sundays and Wednesdays. You can sacrifice your money by paying tithes and supporting world missions. You can even sacrifice your energy and effort by getting involved in some humanitarian relief project. Unfortunately, you can do all these things and still not live in unity with your brothers and sisters in Christ. You can engage in all these religious activities and still not be doing the will of the Father here on earth. That is why under the anointing of God, Samuel tells Saul that "to obey is better than sacrifice" (1 Samuel 15:22). You can only ever fully embrace the mystery of the relational kingdom of heaven and the Christian walk of unity in the body of Christ through the personal discipline of obedience. In fact, Deuteronomy 7:12-13 ties the blessings of God to obeying the commands of God and serving him with all your heart.

The Issue of Servanthood

All of this leads us to the second mysterious and paradoxical word: "servanthood." What is the paradox? Mark states that "whoever wants to become great among you must be your servant, and whoever wants to be first must be slave of all" (Mark 10:43-44). Where is the mystery here? What is this concept that the world has such a hard time understanding? It is simply that the greatest title and honor in the kingdom of God is the unassuming word "servant." Even Jesus Christ, "who being in very nature God, did not consider equality with God something to be used to his own advantage; rather, he made himself nothing by taking on the very nature of a servant" (Philippians 2:6-7).

God the Father—in announcing his son, Jesus Christ—says, "here is my servant whom I have chosen" (Matthew 12:18). All the apostles wore the title of servant gladly. We read it as an introduction to almost every book in the New Testament:

- Paul, a servant of God and an apostle of Jesus Christ" (Titus 1:1)
- Simon Peter, "a servant and apostle of Jesus Christ" (2 Peter 1:1)
- James, "a servant of God and of the Lord Jesus Christ" (James 1:1)
- Jude, "a servant of Jesus Christ and a brother of James" (Jude 1:1)

This title of "servant" and the lifestyle of servanthood is universally the highest honor in the relational kingdom we are to be a part of. Even John, on the island of Patmos as God was making his revelation known, started to bow down to worship at the feet of the angel who had been showing him all the things of heaven and of the future. The angel's response? "Don't do that! I am a fellow servant with you and your fellow prophets and with all who keep the words of the scroll" (Revelation 22:9).

When speaking of Old Testament characters, they were almost always honored by giving them the title of servant. So, we read phrases like "Daniel, servant of the living God" (Daniel 6:20); "For he [God] remembered his holy promise given to his servant Abraham" (Psalm 105:42); and "Moses was faithful as a servant in all God's house" (Hebrews 3:5). Even when speaking of King David as a man after God's own heart, it is noted more than 40 times in the book of Psalms that he was a servant of God.

A good and faithful servant does what his master asks of him. It is no small coincidence that many of the parables of Jesus Christ have something to do with a servant. You cannot even begin to understand the kind of powerful unity that God has in store for his children until you understand the importance and value of service and servanthood. As a fellow believer and as someone involved in this dynamic relational kingdom, I strongly urge you to embrace the word "servant" to be your hallmark and title.

The Issue of Submission

But what does it take to be a servant or to live in obedience? Simply this, submission to the will of another. It is absolutely essential. If you have been in church for any length of time, I would hazard to guess that you have heard many sermons on submission. Unfortunately, often they have been focused on wives submitting to their husbands in a very gender-biased way. Even though in patriarchal societies far too often this has been a way to "keep women in their place," the Bible deals with this issue in a very non-gender-biased way. We must for a few moments address this issue because like it or not, submission is essential for the workings of a healthy strong marital relationship. In fact, it is important for any relationship to be successful. However, to be fair to women, I will have to say that historically men have been very lopsided in their approach to the whole issue of submission in relationships.

This was never more evident to me than in counseling settings where I was working with a group of men who had been abusive to their wives. They were often the first to point out the Bible verses on wives submitting to their husbands. Often, they used the fact that their wives were not submissive in the way that they wanted them to be as a rationalization or justification for their own bad behavior. So whenever this came up, I was quick to point out that in addition to being a counselor, I was also an ordained minister and that I knew a little bit about the verses that they were alluding to. So, I would directly ask them, "What is it about you as a person that allows you to focus on what the Bible has to say about women and submission while totally ignoring all the verses before and after not to mention the entire context of those verses." At this point they would often look at me dumbfounded and ask, "What do you mean?" That was the exact invitation I was looking for, so I would then proceed.

Submission is not something you hold over another person's head so that you can lord it over them. Submission is a gift you give to strengthen relationships. In fact, submission is what makes relationships work. It is the glue that holds committed people together in unity and love. Just ahead of the verse in the Bible that talks about wives submitting to their husbands is the verse that introduces this whole topic. It simply says, "submit to one another out of reverence for Christ" (Ephesians 5:21). In other words, submission is something for everyone. Once that foundation is laid, it then goes on then to say "wives, submit to your husbands as you do to the Lord" (Ephesians 5:22).

I will note here that the Bible is a very gender equitable document.

Unfortunately, it was written in a time and about a culture that was extremely patriarchal. Therefore, you need to pay attention to the difference between what is said about the culture and what God asks of our behavior since they often do not match up. The Bible makes it clear that once we are born again, we are seen as "neither Jew nor Gentile, neither slave or free, nor is there male and female, for you are all one in Christ Jesus" (Galatians 3:28).

As a result, Paul—in writing to the Ephesians—tells wives to submit to their husbands. Living in a very patriarchal society, they already knew what that meant. Paul immediately added, "In this same way, husbands ought to love their wives" (Ephesians 5:28). In what same way? In submission. Paul knowing that they lived in a patriarchal society where the men would be less likely to understand goes on to explain that they should love their wives "just as Christ loved the church and gave himself up for her" (Ephesians 5:25).

But these chapters in the Bible are not just about men and women in marital relationships. The following verses say that children should obey their parents (Ephesians 6:1). In other words, they too should live in submission. Speaking again to the men, Paul said, "Fathers, do not exasperate your children" (Ephesians 6:4). In other words, even though you are the parent and even though you are bigger, wiser, and have more knowledge, sometimes—for the sake of the relationship— you, too, need to submit. Next, Paul stated that slaves should submit to their masters or, in today's terms, that employees should submit to their employers (Ephesians 6:5). But then he turns right around and adds, "And masters, treat your slaves in the same way" (Ephesians 6:9). In what same way? In submission.

God's word points out that "everyone should be subject to the governing authorities" (Romans 13:1) and that you must "submit yourselves, then, to God" (James 4:7). You see, submission is something that we all must do to make relationships work. This is true whether it is our relationships to others or is our relationship to God. At some point we must voluntarily lay aside our own personal selfishness and submit our wills to the interests and desire of others if we are ever going to be connected in relationships.

At this point, I think it is important to briefly address the world's distorted view of submission. Because of how often men involved in domestic violence and alcoholic lifestyles tend to quote the verses on women submitting to their husbands, there has arisen a whole field of pop psychology addressing the phenomenon of co-dependency. In this context, women who submit to their abusive husbands or boy friends are seen as weak individuals who facilitate a troubled lifestyle by desperately clinging to the relationship out of fear and weakness. I know that there are many desperate men and women in terrible situations like those described. I spent many years of my life working at different agencies and even as a director of a sexual abuse program helping men, women, and children turn their abusive relationships around into something more hopeful and positive in their lives. So, I do want to make it perfectly clear that when we talk about submission, we are not talking about co-dependency. Submission should never come from a position of weakness, fear, or necessity. Instead, submission should always come from a position of strength and positive choice.

In meekness, Jesus Christ submitted himself to death on the cross. He was not co-dependent or weak. But rather, he was displaying absolute power and authority under absolute control for the sake of love. His gift of love and submission was given out of a position of strength and choice. Where is the paradox and where is the mystery in submission, you might ask? Although you are a believer, a child of God, and a joint heir with Jesus Christ with all the rights, privileges, power, and authority that come with those titles, to access those privileges, you must become a slave to righteousness—fully embracing a lifestyle of obedience, servanthood, and submission.

In each instance where we see significant men and women of God submitting themselves to someone else, it is for the joy that is set before them. They have become people who understand the whole concept of delayed gratification. They understand that this small investment they are making in the lives of others around them will one day pay great dividends in the kinds of relationships they build with God and others. They understand the power of unity and the means to achieve it. Therefore, if we truly want to experience a radical kingdom life, if we long for a life of continual growth and positive change, if we want to know real power, and if we want to turn the world upside down, then both our words and lifestyles should loudly proclaim that the kingdom of heaven is at hand. Stop being an undercover Christian. Instead learn obedience, servanthood, and submission.

"This then is how you ought to regard us: as servants of Christ and as those entrusted with the mysteries God has revealed. Now it is required that those who have been given a trust must prove faithful."

1 Corinthians 4:1-2

21   **Stewards of the Mystery**

As we have taken the time to explore God the Father's puzzles, we have discovered the mystery of godliness, redemption, his grace, his forgiveness, and his love. As we have delved deeply into the parables of Jesus Christ, the mystery of his kingdom has been revealed, what it means to live a kingdom life has been clarified, and we have been told that to be part of that kingdom, we must bear fruit. Additionally, as we have embraced the paradoxes that are possible only through the empowering of the Holy Spirit, we have learned how to manifest the mystery of Christ in each of us, which is the hope of glory.

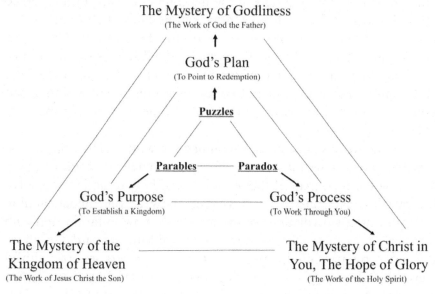

Figure 7: God's Mysteries

We have taken this incredible journey of discovery into the mysteries which had previously been hidden from the foundations of the world, but which now have been revealed to us. Having done so, we must recognize that "from everyone who has been given much, much will be demanded; and from the one who has been entrusted with much, much more will be asked" (Luke 12:48). Therefore, since we have been entrusted with these mysteries that God has revealed, we must now be faithful to apply them to our own lives and then be diligent in passing them on to others. We are charged with the task of "mak[ing] plain to everyone the administration of this mystery, which for ages past was kept hidden in God, who created all things" (Ephesians 3:9). Peter points out that "each of you should use whatever gift you have received to serve others, as faithful stewards of God's grace in its various forms" (1 Peter 4:10).

In proclaiming these mysteries, you need "to pray that God will open the door of utterance to speak the mystery of Christ" (Colossians 4:3), "to open your mouths boldly to make known the mystery of the gospel" (Ephesians 6:19), and "to make all men see what is the fellowship of the mystery which from the beginning of the word was hid in God, who created all things by Christ" (Ephesians 3:9). Not only are you to boldly proclaim the good news of salvation by grace through the sacrifice of Jesus Christ, but as faithful stewards of the mysteries, you must disciple others to do so too. The great commission states, "Therefore, go and make disciples of all nations, baptizing them in the name of the Father and of the Son and of the Holy Spirit and teaching them to obey everything I have commanded you. And surely I am with you always, to the very end of the age" (Matthew 28:19-20).

In order to make disciples, in conjunction with the Holy Spirit who is with us always, we must teach others how to live by paradoxes, how to follow the road map of the parables, and how to notice and solve the puzzles. We must also show them how to find understanding through Christ's revelations of the mysteries, how to fall in step with his plan, and then in turn how to be faithful stewards of those mysteries by passing them on to the next generation of faithful stewards. Ultimately if we are ever to be successful in doing so, we must fully flesh out with our own lives the paradoxes of the kingdom through the power of the Holy Spirit.

A Paradox

Our one God-given right, our only inalienable right, is the power to choose. We like to think that we have many inalienable rights. We in America often talk about the right to life, liberty, and the pursuit of happiness and what it means to have freedom. It is part of our

American enculturation and heritage to believe these things are so. However, even though as born-again Christians we are promised eternal life, we have no guarantee of tomorrow in this earthly life. There are also many strong Christians around the world who do not live in a country where they have individual liberty or freedom. Additionally, while in Christ we can find joy even in difficult circumstances, we are not always free to pursue happiness. We really and truly only have one God-given right, only one freedom; and that is the right to choose.

The paradox is this, that although God gives us that right, he then turns around, steps forcefully into our lives, and tells us what we should choose. He does this because he is all knowing; he knows the end from the beginning. As such he tells us what to choose and then implores us to choose wisely. For example, "This day I call heaven and earth as witnesses against you that I have set before you life and death, blessings and curses. Now choose life, so that you and your children may live and that you may love the LORD your God, listen to his voice, and hold fast to him. For the LORD is your life" (Deuteronomy 30:19).

Therefore, if you really want to be free, become a slave to righteousness; choose life.

Another Paradox

Christ will rule over a kingdom where he has absolute authority, where his will is done on earth as it is in heaven, where every knee will bow and confess that he is Lord to the Glory of God the Father. However, although this kingdom will be based on absolute authority, it will be composed entirely of beings who have free choice and who voluntarily choose to submit to his absolute authority. The only way that is possible is if instead of posturing about personal rights and demanding that you be free to "find yourself," that you willingly choose to submit to a higher authority. If this is ever going to be a reality in your life then you must learn to listen and hear his voice.

So, if you want to live in the kingdom, then die to yourself and learn submission.

Yet Another Paradox

God predestined you to become joint heirs with Jesus Christ. "In him we were also chosen, having been predestined according to the plan of him who works out everything in conformity with the purpose of his will, in order that we, who were the first to hope in Christ, might be for the praise of his glory. And you also were included in Christ when you heard the word of truth, the gospel of your salvation. Having believed, you were marked in him with a seal, the promised Holy Spirit, who is a deposit guaranteeing our inheritance until the redemption of those who are God's possession—to the praise of his glory" (Ephesians 1:11-14). The paradox is this that even though he has predestined you for greatness in him, he will allow you the wide-open path of living your own life and choosing any other destiny no matter how dysfunctional.

So, if you want to find your life, you must first lose it. Choose God's limiting, narrow path instead of your own wide-open options of self-will and self-determination.

Still Yet Another Paradox

When we come to Christ, our path becomes easier. "Come to me, all you who are weary and burdened, and I will give you rest. Take my yoke upon you and learn from me, for I am gentle and humble in heart, and you will find rest for your souls. For my yoke is easy and my burden is light" (Matthew 11:28-30). Even though we know this is true because it was spoken by Jesus Christ, the paradox is this that we must suffer and endure hardships for the kingdom's sake. For example, in the book of Revelation, John introduces himself as "John, your brother and companion in the suffering and kingdom and patient endurance that are ours in Jesus . . ." (Revelation 1:9).

Also as Paul endeavors to be a faithful steward by passing on these things to Timothy, he states, "In the presence of God and of Christ Jesus, who will judge the living and the dead, and in view of his appearing and his kingdom, I give you this charge: preach the word; be prepared in season and out of season; correct, rebuke, and encourage—with great patience and careful instruction. For the time will come when men will not put up with sound doctrine. Instead, to suit their own desires, they will gather around them a great number of teachers to say what their itching ears want to hear. They will turn their ears away from the truth and turn aside to myths. But you, keep your head in all situations, endure hardship, do the work of an evangelist, discharge all the duties of your ministry" (2 Timothy 4:1-5).

So, if you want an easy life of true joy and peace, be willing to learn what great things you must suffer and/or endure for his name's sake; choose his yoke.

The paradoxes we live out by faith are not always easy. Make no mistake; God does not want you to follow him through blind faith. He does not want you to walk unknowingly into this journey and then become disillusioned because of the difficulties you might encounter. Instead, in the King James Version of the Bible he says "Come now, and let us reason together" (Isaiah 1:18). God wants a reasoned faith. He wants you to become a faithful steward of his mystery. But he does not want you to take on this task lightly. The following passage illustrates the seriousness of following Jesus:

"Large crowds were traveling with Jesus, and turning to them, he said, "If anyone comes to me and does not hate father and mother, wife and children, brothers and sisters—yes, even his own life—he cannot be my disciple. And whoever does not carry his cross and follow me cannot be my disciple.

Suppose one of you wants to build a tower. Won't you first sit down and estimate the cost to see if you have enough money to complete it? For if you lay the foundation and are not able to finish it, everyone who sees it will ridicule you, saying, 'This fellow began to build and was not able to finish.'

Or suppose a king is about to go to war against another king. Won't he first sit down and consider whether he is able with ten thousand men to oppose the one coming against him with twenty thousand? If he is not able, he will send a delegation while the other is still a long way off and will ask for terms of peace.

In the same way, any of you who do not give up everything he has cannot be my disciples. Salt is good, but if it loses its saltiness, how can it be made salty again? It is fit neither for the soil nor for the manure pile; it is thrown out. Whoever has ears to hear, let them hear." (Luke 14:25-35)

Being a faithful steward of God's mysteries is so much better than any other option you might choose, but it is not an easy path. It will cost you everything. To be a faithful steward of his mysteries, you must bear fruit. To be a faithful steward of the mysteries, you must go and change your world—one relationship at a time— building a living, unshakable kingdom so that God's will is done first in your life and then in the lives of those around you. You must choose to be an active part of the process of establishing his kingdom so that it may grow to fill the whole earth. Being a faithful steward is a challenge that you could never hope to accomplish on your own. However, because it is a relational kingdom, you have the rest of the body of believers, Jesus Christ, and the power of the Holy spirit, who will all join forces with you to accomplish what seems impossible. "Therefore, since we are receiving a kingdom that cannot be shaken, let us be thankful and so worship God acceptably with reverence and awe" (Hebrews 12:28).

And finally, perhaps this is the greatest paradox of all—that an infinitely creative and all-powerful God whose ways are higher than our ways, whose love is beyond measure, and whose riches are unsearchable is deeply and passionately invested in the life journey of an insignificant human being made lower than the angels with all the flaws, frailty, shortcomings, imperfections, foibles, and sins that so easily beset you. His greatest joy is seeing you become a servant and seeing you as one entrusted with the mysteries that God has revealed. Why? Because he knows that it is not possible for you to do so on your own. To the extent that you do become a faithful steward, it means that he was allowed to share the journey with you. In your weakness, he was allowed to show himself strong. In your inadequacies, he was allowed to become a very present help in time of trouble. In your battles, his mind was allowed to be in you. Through all your efforts, he was allowed to be your source. He walked along side you each step of the way. In this dynamic relational kingdom, he was allowed to have an intimate relationship with you. After all, when you are truly, madly, and deeply in love with someone, sometimes there is nothing better than just holding their hand and walking together.

Because God is truly, madly, and deeply in love with you, he wants to hold your hand every step of the way. Ultimately, if we are ever going to reciprocate that love, then we must become faithful stewards of the mysteries of the kingdom. Why? Because the journey that he is on is one that involves building a living, unshakeable kingdom where his Father's will is done on earth just as it is in heaven. If you truly love him and want to hold his hand and walk with him, it means that you are also intentional about going in that direction. In relationship with Jesus Christ, you are helping to build a living unshakable kingdom.

Therefore, as faithful stewards of the mysteries of the kingdom, you should constantly be about the business of letting others know that . . .

Jesus wants them to see answers everywhere they look,
but only if they are looking.

He wants them to hear the clues and their meanings,
but only if they are listening.

He wants them to understand the mysteries of his kingdom,
but only if they want to be part of the kingdom.

And he desperately wants to point them in the right direction,
but only if they choose to go on the journey with him.

Epilogue

"The secret things belong to the Lord our God, but the things that are revealed belong to us and to our children forever, that we may do all the words of this law."

Deuteronomy 29:29

Epilogue
Making the Mystery Known

If you have the faith to believe that these mysteries have been revealed through God's Word and that they are relevant for your life and for today, then you must take the next step and do something about what you believe. How will you walk out your beliefs? Will you choose to allow God's revelation to impact your everyday actions? Furthermore, now having added this new knowledge about the mysteries of godliness, the kingdom of heaven, and Christ in you the hope of glory, I challenge you to also add self-control. How will you discipline yourself to implement the things you now know in your own life, and how will you discipline yourself to implement the things you now know for the sake of those around you?

Since, as we have learned, this is all about a relational kingdom, how will you choose to allow the mysteries to impact your relationships? Will you be a servant to others, obeying God's voice in your own life for the sake of the kingdom and in the lives of others in your sphere of influence? If, as we have discovered, you are the process by which God is building his kingdom, what role do you in particular have to play in the advancement of his cause? What specific and unique puzzles and mysteries might God whisper into your life? When he does, will you listen and obey?

Finally, if you dare to step up to the challenge of being a faithful steward of the mysteries of God, then how will you pass this information on to the next generation? Not only must you be diligent to share this knowledge and growth process with your children and your children's children, but you must also reach out to as many others as you can and welcome them into this unique relational kingdom by demonstrating the love and unity that is the hallmark of the kingdom. As such, you should "pray also . . . that whenever [you] open [your] mouth, words may be given [you] so that [you] will fearlessly make known the mystery of the gospel" (Ephesians 6:19).

Dr. Randall Feller, a
Minister, Psychologist, and
Marriage & Family Therapist
from Tulsa, Oklahoma is a
Senior Professor in the
Behavioral Science Department
at Oral Roberts University.
He is the husband of Diana and
father of Laura and Nathan

Made in the USA
Middletown, DE
29 July 2022

God invites you on an epic journey as a faithful steward of his mysteries.

When seeking to understand God's larger plan, he speaks of mysteries and hidden things. He purposely speaks through puzzles, parables, riddles, and paradox. Even so, he implores you to take up the challenge and travel with him on an amazing adventure of discovery. This is not an exploration that is for the faint of heart. It is a selective process designed only for those who will seek first the kingdom and who will search for God with all their heart. It is a journey that involves understanding God's secret wisdom, his hidden knowledge, and his fantastic mysteries.

We speak of God's secret wisdom, a wisdom that has been hidden and that God destined for our glory before time began." (I Corinthians 2:7-8)

Even though God's communication with mankind often appears fuzzy or cloudy, as if shrouded in secrecy, he invites you to become actively involved and understand more of the mystery of his kingdom and what he wants for your life.

What does God want?

He wants you to see answers everywhere you look,
but only if you're looking.

He wants you to hear the clues and their meanings,
but only if you're listening.

He wants you to understand the mystery of his kingdom,
but only if you want to be part of the kingdom.

He wants to point you in the right direction,
but only if you choose to go on the journey with him.

ISBN 979-8-9866261-0-9

9 798986 626109

90000>